Vegetarian Cooking for People with Allergies

Raphael Rettner, D.C.

Book Publishing Company
Summertown, Tennessee

Cover design: Sheryl Karas
Interior design: Warren C. Jefferson

Printed in the U.S. by Book Publishing Company
P.O. Box 99
Summertown, TN 38483

ISBN 1-57067-045-5

Rettner, Raphael, D.C., 1963-
    Vegetarian cooking for people with allergies / Raphael Rettner, D.C.
        p. cm.
    Includes index.
        ISBN 1-57067-045-5 (alk. paper)
    1. Food allergy--Diet therapy--Recipes. 2. Vegetarian cookery.
    I. TItle.
    RC596.R48 1997
    616.97'50654--dc21   97-30405
                                                          CIP

This book contains a brief overview of the causes of food allergies and related treatments. The opinions expressed are based on the experience and training of the author. If you have a medical condition, please consult with your doctor before making changes in your diet.

Calculations for the nutritional analyses in this book are based on the average number of servings listed with the recipes and the average amount of an ingredient, if a range is called for. Calculations are rounded up to the nearest gram. If two options for an ingredient are listed, the first one is used. Not included are fat used for frying, unless the amount is specified in the recipe, optional ingredients, or serving suggestions.

Table of Contents

INTRODUCTION

As a chiropractor in private practice for over ten years, I have successfully helped hundreds of patients suffering with food and airborne allergies become allergy-free. My patients get well without the use of medications, allergy shots, or rotation diets. This is only possible by treating the underlying cause of the allergy instead of just treating the symptoms.

Allergies to milk, wheat, and eggs cover at least 90% of what is seen in most allergists' offices. In the past, when I have taken allergic patients off wheat and dairy products, their typical reaction was, "There's nothing left to eat." This concern is very real. Wheat and dairy products are present at almost every meal in the form of bread, cakes, cheese, crackers, milk, cookies, and pasta. You can also find wheat where you don't expect it, such as in soy sauce. Even so-called "non-dairy" substitutes and "imitation" milk products contain casein, a milk protein. I wrote this allergy-free cookbook so that the allergic patient could live a normal life and enjoy a healthful vegetarian diet without the most common food allergens, and their entire family could enjoy favorite foods without craving the offending ingredients that must be avoided.

The Causes and Symptoms of Food Allergies

Allergies are generally thought of as a malfunction of the immune system: the body has a reaction to a substance which is normally harmless. According to my clinical experience, I have found this to be only half true. The allergic person's immune system sees a normally harmless food as a dangerous invader similar to a bacteria or virus. The body produces quantities of antibodies to fight off this perceived invader, which causes symptoms associated with allergic reactions: hives, respiratory distress, and digestive problems such as diarrhea and indigestion.

I have found that most people get allergies because of stress, usually due to unexpressed anger from some sort of emotional stress, a bad night's sleep, being overworked, or from environmental stress. When the emotions that result from this stress become repressed instead of released, blood flow to the digestive organs is reduced. This lack of blood flow, in turn, can cause depressed functioning of the immune system.

Interestingly enough, food allergies are related to cravings. If you crave a food (such as wheat or dairy products) and you eat it all the time, there's a good chance that you're allergic to it. Science has tried to explain this allergic addiction phenomenon, but has been unsuccessful to date. One theory is that certain foods affect various neurotransmitters, the substances that send nerve impulses between the neurons in the brain. One example of a neurotransmitter is serotonin, which can affect one's mood. Foods high in carbohydrates will raise serotonin levels. Stressful emotions, such as fear, have been found to lower serotonin levels. Therefore, when you are under stress, you may crave foods that raise your serotonin levels, even if you're allergic to them. There's also a substance in the brain called enkephalin, which acts like a narcotic. When it is released due to stress, you may feel compelled to compensate for it by eating foods you're allergic to. In these situations children tend to crave peanut butter, pizza, milk, and sugar. Women tend to crave chocolate, pastries, yogurt, and coffee, while men will go for cheese, beer, and beef. Chocolate cravings may be due to a magnesium deficiency, while a craving for beer may be caused by a yeast allergy. Foods that you crave are the worst ones to eat, as cravings are the strongest indicator of food allergies.

There are many symptoms related to food allergies. If you're constantly bloated and have gas all the time, there's a good chance you're allergic to something you're eating. It's normal to have more energy after eating; feeling tired after eating is an indication of a possible food allergy. Gaining excess water weight is also the result of reactions to food allergens. After avoiding food allergens, many people lose weight without any change in caloric intake.

Symptoms of allergies in children may include hyperactivity, migraine headaches, obesity, arthritis, and asthma. Learning disabilities in children and lack of coordination may also be seen. These can all be caused by allergies and are often treated by the preservative-free Feingold diet.* Children also may have ear infections, congested sinuses, diarrhea, fatigue, sleep disorders, stomach aches, and acne—all due to allergies. Migraine headaches in children may be due to an allergy to wheat, dairy products, eggs, chocolate, sugar, yeast, citrus, red meat, or corn (in adults, foods such as red wine, tea, and coffee may be the cause). If you suspect your child has food allergies, eliminate the foods

---

*Feingold, B. *The Feingold Diet for Hyperactive Children*. New York:Random House.

your child craves (as well as the most common allergen foods) for five days. Then add one food back into their diet at a time, and look for any noticeable symptom.

Since allergic reactions to foods can cause a wide range of discomforts, you may want to note the following list of possible symptoms:

Digestive: Indigestion (vomiting, gas, nausea), constipation, gall bladder pain, heartburn, abdominal pain, gastrointestinal bleeding, hemorrhoids, gastric ulcers, gastric pain, colitis;

Psychological: Depression, nervous and emotional instability;

Respiratory: Asthma, sinus congestion;

Dermatological: Hives, canker sores;

Miscellaneous: Recurrent headaches, migraines, high blood pressure, heart attack and angina, epilepsy, irritability, diabetes, conjunctivitis, abnormal tiredness, underweight and overweight.

Often, medications are taken unnecessarily for conditions caused by food allergies when a simple test could determine whether allergies are the problem.

Foods That Commonly Cause Allergic Reactions

The most common food allergies are to wheat, dairy products, the nightshade family (eggplant, bell peppers, tomatoes, potatoes, cayenne, and paprika), citrus, chocolate, eggs, corn, soy (including tofu, miso, tempeh, etc.), and peanuts. Wheat and wheat products are present in a large percentage of foods consumed in the U.S. today. Some researchers believe that because we eat such a large quantity of wheat, the digestive enzymes we have that break down wheat can become exhausted and lead to a food allergy. Other researchers feel wheat allergies are due to sensitivities to gluten or reactions to aflatoxins (a mold that grows on wheat). I feel these are only superficial causes. In my experience, I've found the deeper underlying cause is emotional stress. And while you work to relieve the source of your stress, you can remove offending foods from your diet.

Bread is the most common form of wheat in our diet, but biscuits, crackers, muffins, pancakes, popovers, pretzels, and rolls contain it as well. Different kinds of breads may appear to be wheat-free, but may not be, such as corn gluten, graham, pumpernickel, rye (rye products are not entirely free of wheat), and soy-wheat. Some common brands of breakfast cereal that contain wheat are bran flakes, corn flakes, cream of wheat, farina, Grapenuts, puffed wheat, Rice Krispies, Shredded Wheat, Wheatena, and other malted cereals. Beverages and beverage ingredients that can contain wheat are coco malt, beer, gin (any drink with grain neutral spirits), malted milk, Ovaltine, Postum, and whiskey. Wheat is a common ingredient in cakes, cookies, doughnuts, pies, chocolate candy and candy bars, and puddings, as well as dumplings, all pasta products, and zweiback and rusk. Look for it also in bouillon cubes, fried foods that are breaded, gravies, ice cream cones, matzohs, and mayonnaise. Always check for wheat or wheat flour on the list of ingredients for any product you buy.

Nightshade vegetables (tomatoes, eggplant, peppers, etc.) are commonly found in Mexican and Italian cooking. Eggplant Parmesan, marinara sauce, antipasto, and salsa are a few examples of this.

There are many delicious substitutes for foods that might disagree with you: rice cakes, rice cookies, rice flour bread and other wheat-free breads, and soy, rice, and almond milk. Rice milk ice cream, soy or almond cheeses, and unsweetened frozen fruit popsicles are alternatives to desserts made from cow's milk.

Candida Albicans and Food Allergies

Yeasts are one of a number of organisms whose characteristics are neither wholly plant nor animal. One family of yeast, Candida albicans, normally lives on the mucus membranes of the digestive tract and vagina. These are the yeasts that cause bread to rise and fruit to ferment into wine. We eat them, drink them, and breathe them. Normally these yeasts live in harmony with us throughout our lives. When your immune system is strong, they aren't able to break through into your deeper tissues or bloodstream and make you sick. However, under certain conditions these yeasts can multiply to the extent that their presence can cause your health to deteriorate. At that point, you are no longer supporting a parasite whose presence is inconsequential; instead, you have developed a Candida albicans infection. An overgrowth of Candida can cause multiple food allergies by causing irritation to the gastrointestinal tract. If you eat a particular food and experience extreme bloating and abdominal pain afterwards, that food is probably aggravating a Candida problem.

The extensive and liberal use of antibiotics, birth control pills, and steroid drugs, as well as a highly refined carbohydrate diet, all contribute to this unfortunate shift in the balance between man and yeast.

Also heavily implicated are increases in environmental pollutants, poor nutrition, destructive lifestyles, and stress.

When you take antibiotics, especially if you take them repeatedly, many of the friendly germs in your body (especially those in your digestive tract) are wiped out. Since yeasts aren't harmed by these antibiotics, they spread out and raise large families. Only a few antifungal agents (such as nystatin) are available for the treatment of systemic yeast overgrowth and are obtainable only by prescription. Treatment with these drugs, especially for extended periods, can lead to problems with intolerance or the development of resistant organisms during the course of therapy.

It should also be recognized that Candida can exist in two states: a yeast-like form and a mycelial fungal form. In its mycelial stage, long, root-like growths penetrate mucous tissues. This is a particularly troublesome form which may contribute to particularly severe Candida infections in some individuals.

Traditional & Non-Traditional Allergy Treatments

The traditional medical treatment for allergies has been allergy shots—injecting small doses of the allergen and gradually increasing the dosage to produce an acquired immunity. These shots are like vaccinations. They're painful and often very expensive. They only work about a third of the time, and there's always a possibility of an accidental overdose causing anaphylactic shock, possible kidney failure, and even death. And worse, getting an allergy shot is just like sweeping something under a rug. Instead of dealing with the cause of the allergy, allergy shots only relieve the symptoms.

Another traditional treatment is nasal sprays or decongestants. These sprays can irritate the mucous lining of the nose and often lose their effectiveness over a short period of time. Again, this form of treatment only addresses the symptoms of an allergy, not the cause.

Finally, there are steroid medications. These are given to supplement the adrenal glands, which play an important role in fighting allergies. However, the constant use of steroids ends up depleting the adrenal glands instead.

The traditional procedure used to determine an allergy is the administration of a skin test, as well as a blood test called the RAAST or Radio Allergies Absorbent Test. The RAAST measures allergy antibodies. The greater the reaction, the higher the RAAST score will be. Foods that score 2, 3, or 4 on the RAAST are avoided for 2 months and then rotated back into the diet at a rate of one per week. This is a lengthy process and often very disruptive to the patient and their family.

Foods may also be tested using a rotation diet. Starting with some of the foods most likely to cause a food allergy, a single different food is eaten at each meal for several days: bread for breakfast, eggs for lunch, and tomatoes for dinner, for instance. A note is made of any symptoms experienced. Then a new group of foods is tried. If a food allergy is present, sooner or later a particular food will trigger symptoms.

Muscle Testing

With muscle testing (sometimes referred to as *applied kinesiology*), the doctor can test which foods the patient is allergic to by using a muscle response test. I have found this method to be quick, reliable, and inexpensive for patients. The large pectoral muscle that runs from the top of the arm into the chest (the pectoralis major clavicular) is a convenient muscle to use for this test. The practitioner tests to see if this muscle is strong. If this is the case, it can be considered a "strong indicator muscle." To perform the test, the practitioner has the patient chew the suspected food allergen slightly until it mixes with saliva. It's important not to swallow the food until after the test. The practitioner then retests the strong indicator muscle. If the muscle now appears weak, the patient is probably sensitive or allergic to that particular food. The muscle is still as strong as ever. The appearance of weakness is caused by the food allergen slowing the response time from the brain to the muscle, much like a busy signal. It's also similar to feeling weak after tasting spoiled food.

You can also do a pulse test to confirm your findings. Count your pulse for one minute just after waking, but before getting out of bed in the morning; just before each meal; three times after each meal at half-hour intervals; and just before retiring. All the pulse counts should be made sitting except when you awake; this is made before you sit up. Record the time you eat each meal, and continue the pulse-dietary records for two or three days, eating three meals a day.

Then make single-food tests of the most common allergic foods for two or more days, beginning after the "before rising" count in the morning and continuing for 12 hours. Eat a small portion of a different single food every two hours—for example, a slice of bread or a glass of milk or juice. Count your pulse just before you eat this food, 15 minutes later, and every 15 minutes for the next hour and a half. (Don't eat any food that is known to disagree with you, just ones that you suspect.) If your pulse increases by 12-16 beats per minute any time during this period, note which food you ate most recently and write it down. If any foods raised your pulse, completely eliminate them from your diet for five days. Then add back each food one at a time to see whether or not it causes an allergic reaction. Also write down any symptoms you may experience after eating the food, such as tiredness, bloating, irritability, etc. (See the symptoms list on page 6.) Be aware that the pulse test is not conclusive and does not work for everyone.

Most Common Allergy-Causing Foods

Wheat
Dairy milk and cheese
Eggs
Corn
Yeast
Chocolate
Coffee

Vegetables:
Asparagus
Beets
Bell peppers
Cabbage
Carrots
Cayenne
Eggplant
Onions
Spinach
Sweet potatoes
Tomatoes
White potatoes

Legumes:
Beans and peas
Peanuts
Soybeans
   (tofu, tempeh,
   tamari, miso)

Fruits:
Apples
Bananas
Grapes
Grapefruit
Lemons
Melons
Oranges
Pineapples
Plums
Strawberries

Allergy Correction Technique

Twelve years ago I was allergic to wheat, dairy products, peanuts, and eggs. After eating them I felt tired, depressed, and bloated. It would ruin my day. I thought that was how you were supposed to feel after eating. After several years of suffering, I received an allergy correction treatment from a chiropractor in San Diego. After one treatment, I went out and had an egg salad sandwich on whole wheat bread, a peanut candy for dessert, and had no reaction whatsoever.

The Allergy Correction Technique directly addresses organ and energy imbalances. This eliminates the root cause of the allergic reaction. In this technique, food allergens are muscle tested on the first visit, and most food allergies are usually corrected on the next one or two visits. The success of this technique lies in its ability to release the underlying emotional cause of the allergy, which then increases blood flow and improves immune function. To learn more about this valuable method, you may order my video *Allergy Correction Technique* by calling 1-800-236-6899 or my office at 510-526-4394 and 415-383-8260. For more information on other videos, see page 144.

Acid and Alkaline Fruits and Vegetables

Richard Powers, Ph.D., a nutritionist from Baltimore, Maryland, specializes in the statistical analysis and correlation of blood types as they relate to food allergies. He has found that many people with type "O" blood are especially allergic to acid fruits and vegetables. Acid vegetables include bell peppers, beets, eggplant, hot peppers, rhubarb, onions, garlic, raw spinach, and tomatoes. Acid fruits include lemons, limes, oranges, pineapples, cranberries, strawberries, and grapefruit.

Good alkaline vegetables to eat if you have problems with acid foods are zucchini, cucumbers, squash, lettuce, parsley, romaine, spinach, bean sprouts, yams, potatoes, carrots, jicama, and broccoli. Alkaline fruits are papayas, mangos, melons, plums, cherries, grapes, guavas, persimmons, apricots, nectarines, tangerines, figs, apples, blueberries, bananas, kiwis, and prunes.

Food Allergies and Arthritis

Arthritis is often caused by allergies to cayenne pepper, paprika, wheat, dairy products, eggplant, bell pepper, tomatoes, potatoes, meat, fish, fowl, salt, or sugar. For recovery, eat a diet of whole grains and green leafy vegetables. Quinoa and rice are the best grains to use. Use sesame seeds, sunflower seeds, and pumpkin seeds sparingly. The most beneficial fruits and vegetables are watercress, yams, celery, parsley, garlic, comfrey, endive, bananas, and pineapples.

There are also a number of good therapies that are beneficial to arthritis sufferers:

1. Rheumatoid arthritis is very responsive to vegetable juice therapy. Repeated juice fasts of 4 to 6 weeks are recommended; between fasts, diet plans are followed which utilize the above recommended foods. The alkaline action of raw juices dissolves the accumulation of deposits around the joints and in other tissues. A combination of carrot, celery, and red beet juice is specific for arthritis.
2. Taking 6 to 8 tablets of bromelin (pineapple enzyme) helps reduce or eliminate swelling and inflammation in the soft tissues and joints affected by rheumatoid arthritis.
3. Alternate both hot and cold showers, done morning and evening.
4. Follow regular massage and exercises recommended by your health professional.
5. Chiropractic adjustments on the affected joints can be effective in relieving the pain of arthritis.

A Note About Whole Grain Flour

A number of the recipes in this book call for the use of whole grain flour. You can use any grain flour that is wheat-free, such as amaranth, barley, buckwheat, corn, millet, oat, quinoa, rice, tapioca, and teff. Kamut and spelt are ancient forms of cultivated wheat that can also be tolerated by some people with wheat allergies. Try different flours until you find one you particularly like, or experiment with different combinations of flours.

Recipe Symbols

The following symbols on the recipe pages show whether the recipe is free of various foods or food groups:

No Wheat   No Dairy Products   No Eggs   No Corn   No Citrus   No Soy   No Nightshade Vegetables

Breakfast

Breakfast Ideas

Spring & Summer

Choice of:
- Fresh fruit in season or fruit juice: apple, apricot, grapefruit, papaya, peach, pear, pineapple, orange
- Quick cereal: Crispy brown rice flakes, corn flakes, or oat bran flakes—with almond milk, rice milk, or soymilk

Fall & Winter

Choice of:
- Oatmeal, millet, or brown rice cereal
- Sweet potato with non-dairy margarine or vegetable oil and cinnamon
- Mochi (cakes of pounded cooked sweet rice)
- Buckwheat pancakes with pure maple syrup and non-dairy margarine

Coffee Substitute

Roast the grain or seeds on a baking sheet at 500°F for approximately 30 minutes, or until dry and very dark brown. Stir occasionally and check often. When cool, put through a grinder or mill, and grind coarsely like coffee. Use 1 tablespoon per cup to brew.

Garbanzo beans (chick-peas), sunflower seeds, whole feed barley or oats

Per cup: Calories 32, Protein 1 g, Fat 1 g, Carbohydrates 4 g

Date Shake

Yield: 2 servings

Blend all the ingredients until smooth in a blender.

1 cup chopped, pitted dates
1 teaspoon vanilla
1 ripe banana, sliced
2 cups rice or almond milk

Per serving: Calories 376, Protein 8 g, Fat 5 g, Carbohydrates 75 g

Tofu Rancheros

Yield: 4 servings

Serve this hearty Southwestern breakfast dish with chamomile (manzanilla) tea.

2 tablespoons oil or non-dairy
   margarine
4 corn tortillas

Heat the oil in a frying pan, and fry the tortillas on both sides until limp. An alternative is to steam them or toast them in a toaster oven.

1 cup soft tofu, crumbled (½ lb.)
1-2 cups cooked black beans
½ avocado, sliced
Cilantro, chopped

Fry the tofu and cooked black beans together until hot, then spoon onto each tortilla. Serve with slices of avocado and a garnish of fresh cilantro.

Per serving: Calories 301, Protein 12 g, Fat 14 g, Carbohydrates 32 g

Soups

Chilled Cucumber-Dill Soup

Yield: 1 serving

This soup features English cucumbers, which are longer than the standard American cucumber you are used to seeing in salads. If you have problems digesting cucumbers, English cucumbers are for you.

1½ cups rice milk
½ English cucumber

Chill the rice milk in the freezer for 15 minutes. Put the cucumber through a juicer. Combine the cucumber juice and rice milk in a blender.

1 tablespoon fresh dill weed,
  or 1 teaspoon dry dill weed

Pour into a bowl and top with the dill weed.

Per serving: Calories 66, Protein 2 g, Fat 0 g, Carbohydrates 14 g

Chilled Fruit Soup

Yield: 4 servings

Rinse the fruit and remove the seeds. Put the fruit through a juicer, then place the juiced mixture in a blender with the water, arrowroot, fructose, and cinnamon.

½ lb. peaches (1¼ cups)
½ lb. tart red plums (1 cup)
½ lb. cherries (1½ cups)
3 cups water
1 teaspoon arrowroot, dissolved in
    3 tablespoons water
½ cup fructose, or to taste
½ teaspoon cinnamon

Serve in individual bowls topped with soy sour cream or Tofu Whipped Cream, if desired.

Soy sour cream or Tofu Whipped Cream, p. 127 (optional)

Per serving: Calories 188, Protein 1 g, Fat 0 g, Carbohydrates 44 g

Cuban Black Bean Soup

Yield: 4 to 6 servings

1 cup dried black beans, soaked
  overnight, rinsed, and drained
2½-3 cups water or stock
1 cup chopped onions
2 tablespoons apple cider vinegar
2 teaspoons finely chopped garlic
½ teaspoon ground cumin
1 bay leaf
Sea salt and black pepper, to taste

Crockpot Method: Place the beans in a crockpot with 2½ cups water or stock. Use the setting recommended by the manufacturer of your cooker for cooking beans, and cook 6 to 8 hours. One hour before serving, add the onions and remaining spices to the beans in the pot. Taste for seasoning and thin with additional water or stock, if desired. Remove the bay leaf and purée the soup in a blender or food processor.

Stovetop Method: Bring the soaked beans to a boil in 3 cups of water or stock. Lower the heat and simmer for 1 hour. Add the onions and remaining spices to the soup, and cook for another ½ hour. Remove the bay leaf and purée the soup in a blender or food processor. Thin with additional water or stock, if desired.

Per serving: Calories 125, Protein 7 g, Fat 0 g, Carbohydrates 23 g

Dried Fruit Soup

Yield: 8 servings

Soak the dried fruit with the cinnamon stick overnight in the warm water. In the morning, strain out the fruit and save the soaking liquid. Remove the prune pits and cinnamon stick.

1 cup prunes
1 cup dried apricots
1 stick cinnamon
2 quarts warm water

Add the liquid sweetener to the soaking liquid. Mix the arrowroot with a little cold water, and add it to the liquid. Boil for a few minutes to thicken. Add all the fruit, and let the soup stand until cool. Chill in the refrigerator.

2 tablespoons liquid sweetener
1½ tablespoons arrowroot
3 unpeeled organic apples, diced

Per serving: Calories 146, Protein 1 g, Fat 0 g, Carbohydrates 35 g

French Onion Soup

Yield: 4 servings

2 medium Spanish onions, thinly sliced
6 cups water
2 cloves garlic, pressed

¼ cup wheat-free tamari, or to taste
Sea salt and black pepper, to taste
2 tablespoons Herbamare seasoning
3 tablespoons rice polishings
4 slices whole grain bread, toasted and sliced into croutons
¼ lb. sliced soy cheese

Steam the onions until softened, but still firm. Bring the 6 cups of water to a boil. Add the steaming water, onions, and garlic, and simmer for 10 minutes.

Add the tamari, sea salt, black pepper, and Herbamare. Add the rice polishings and transfer the soup to 4 individual earthen pots or soup bowls. Float the toasted croutons and sliced cheese on top. Heat in a moderate oven to melt the cheese.

Per serving: Calories 152, Protein 11 g, Fat 4 g, Carbohydrates 17 g

Greek Bean Soup

Yield: 6 servings

Crockpot Method: Place the soaked beans and celery in a crockpot with the 3 cups water. Use the setting recommended by the manufacturer of your cooker for cooking beans, and cook 6 to 8 hours. Add the carrot, onion, garlic, and seasonings 1 hour before serving. You may stir in the miso just before serving for additional flavor.

Stovetop Method: Place the soaked beans in a soup pot with the 3 cups water. Bring to a boil, lower the heat, and simmer for ½ hour. Add the celery, carrot, onion, garlic, and seasonings, and simmer for another 45 minutes. Remove from the heat and stir in the miso for additional flavor.

1 cup white or cannelini beans, soaked overnight, rinsed, and drained
3 cups water
2 stalks celery with their leaves, diced
1 carrot, diced
1 medium onion, chopped
1-2 cloves garlic, pressed
Herbamare seasoning, to taste
1 teaspoon dried oregano, or 1 tablespoon fresh oregano
1 tablespoon miso (optional)

Per serving: Calories 101, Protein 5 g, Fat 0 g, Carbohydrates 19 g

Hot and Sour Soup

Yield: 4 servings

This recipe features several unusual, but delicious, Oriental ingredients, available in specialty food stores or health food stores. A little toasted sesame oil imparts a wonderful flavor without adding a lot of calories.

¼ cup dried Chinese black mushrooms

Soak the dried mushrooms in very hot water for 20 minutes, and drain.

¼ cup carrots
¼ cup zucchini
¼ cup bamboo shoots (optional)
2 cups water
2 cups soup stock
¼ cup spinach
½ cup tofu, cut into cubes or strips

Slice the mushrooms, carrots, zucchini, and bamboo shoots into long, thin strips. Bring the water to a boil, and add the soup stock. Turn down the heat to low, then add the sliced vegetables, spinach, and tofu. Cook for 10 minutes.

2 tablespoons apple cider vinegar
2 tablespoons wheat-free tamari
1½ tablespoons Chinese hot pepper sauce
¼ teaspoon cayenne pepper
¼ teaspoon toasted sesame oil (optional)

In a small bowl, mix the apple cider vinegar, tamari, and Chinese hot pepper sauce. Add to the soup broth, and cook for 3 minutes. Stir together the cayenne pepper and toasted sesame oil. Add to the soup and serve immediately.

Per serving: Calories 42, Protein 3 g, Fat 1 g, Carbohydrates 4 g

Lentil Soup

Yield: 4 servings

Bring 3 cups of water to a boil in a saucepan, and add the lentils, carrots, onion, garlic, lemon juice (if using), gingerroot, Herbamare, and black pepper; turn the heat to low. Simmer for 1 hour and serve.

1 cup dried lentils
2 carrots, sliced
1 onion, sliced
2 cloves garlic, pressed
3 tablespoons lemon juice (optional)
1 teaspoon sliced fresh gingerroot
1 teaspoon Herbamare seasoning, or to taste
¼ teaspoon black pepper

Per serving: Calories 173, Protein 10 g, Fat 0 g, Carbohydrates 32 g

Spicy Indian Lentil Soup

Prepare the following spices and add them to the Lentil Soup for an authentic Indian dish.

Roast the coriander seeds and cinnamon in a dry frying pan for 3 minutes over medium heat, stirring constantly. Remove from the heat and let cool. Purée the cooled spices in a blender with the coriander leaves and ¼ cup water.

1 tablespoon coriander seeds
½ teaspoon ground cinnamon
2 tablespoons fresh coriander leaves (cilantro)

Heat the oil over medium heat, stir in the cumin and black mustard seeds, and sauté until the seeds begin to sputter (be careful not to burn them).

1 tablespoon oil
1½ teaspoons cumin seeds
1½ teaspoons black mustard seeds

Remove from the heat and stir in the turmeric, fenugreek, and asafoetida. Add to the cooking lentils 1 hour before serving, and cook until the lentils are soft.

½ teaspoon turmeric
¼ teaspoon ground fenugreek (optional)
¼ teaspoon asafoetida or hing (optional)

Minestrone

Yield: about 10 cups

½ cup dried lima, kidney, pinto, or black beans, soaked overnight, rinsed, and drained

½ cup dried garbanzo beans, soaked overnight, rinsed, and drained

2½-3 cups water

4 cups grated fresh tomatoes, or 1 (28-oz.) can tomatoes with their juice, or 1 (6-oz.) can tomato paste and 3 cups vegetable stock (which may include 1 [11½-oz.] can tomato or V-8 juice)

1 onion, finely chopped

1½ cups chopped celery

1½ cups fresh chopped Italian parsley

Herbamare seasoning, to taste

Dash cayenne pepper

1-2 bay leaves

½ cup cooked barley

1½ cups wheat-free pasta

2 cups chopped mixed vegetables: carrots, eggplant or zucchini, broccoli, potatoes, green beans, green peppers, cabbage, or peas

1 teaspoon oregano

2 teaspoons basil

½ teaspoon rosemary

Crockpot Method: Place the soaked beans in a crockpot, and cover with 2½ cups water. Use the setting recommended by the manufacturer of your cooker for cooking beans, and cook 6 to 8 hours.

Add the tomatoes or tomato paste and stock, onion, celery, parsley, Herbamere, pepper, and bay leaves. Add the barley, pasta, mixed vegetables, herbs, and garlic at least 1 hour before serving the soup. The leafy greens should be added to the pot just 5 minutes before serving. (Don't count them as part of the 2 cups mixed vegetables.) Stir well to combine all the ingredients, and adjust the seasonings to taste. If you like, garnish each bowl with a spoonful of rice polishings. (It tastes just like grated Parmesan cheese.)

Stovetop Method: Use 1 cup total of the dried lima, kidney, pinto, or black beans (a mixture of beans is fine), but not the garbanzo beans unless they are already cooked. (If using garbanzos, add 1½ cups cooked garbanzos at the end of the cooking time.) Place the soaked beans in a soup pot along with 3 cups water, the tomatoes or tomato paste and stock, onion, celery, parsley, garlic, seasoning, pepper, and bay leaves. Bring to a boil, then reduce the heat and simmer for 1 hour. Add the pasta, mixed vegetables, herbs, and garlic, and cook 20 more minutes. Add the leafy greens and cooked barley, and simmer 5 more minutes.

1-5 cloves garlic, crushed

1 cup chopped fresh spinach or other leafy greens

Rice polishings, for garnish (optional)

Per serving: Calories 138, Protein 4 g, Fat 1 g, Carbohydrates 28 g

Mock Chicken Soup

Yield: 6 to 8 servings

1 medium onion, chopped
2 stalks celery with leaves, chopped
2 carrots, chopped
1 parsley root, chopped

Steam the vegetables until they are tender; save the steaming water.

3 quarts water, vegetable stock, or water from soaking seeds for sprouting
2 tablespoons vegetarian chicken-style broth powder

Bring the 3 quarts water to a boil in a large pot, and add the chicken-style broth powder.

¼ teaspoon ground ginger
¼ teaspoon chopped fresh dill or dill seeds
Several sprigs parsley, minced
1 bay leaf
Sea salt and black pepper, to taste

Add the vegetables and seasonings, and simmer for 15 minutes.

Per serving: Calories 29, Protein 1 g, Fat 0 g, Carbohydrates 5 g

Mushroom Barley Soup

Yield: 8 servings

Bring the 2½ quarts of water to a boil. Add the barley, broth powder, parsley, onions, carrot, celery, garlic, and mushrooms, and simmer for 1½ hours.

2½ quarts water
1 cup whole barley, washed
4 tablespoons vegetable broth powder
2 sprigs parsley, chopped
1-2 onions, chopped
1 carrot, diced
2 celery stalks, diced
1-2 cloves garlic, minced
1 lb. mushrooms, chopped

Add the seasonings and serve.

1½ teaspoons sea salt
1 teaspoon kelp, or to taste
½ teaspoon dill weed
Black pepper, to taste

Per serving: Calories 73, Protein 2 g, Fat 0 g, Carbohydrates 15 g

Scotch Broth

Yield: 6 to 8 servings

4 cups water
2 carrots, diced
2 onions, diced
2 stalks celery, diced
1 turnip, diced
1 leek, sliced
¼ cup chopped parsley
¼ cup chopped kale

Bring the 4 cups of water to a boil while steaming the vegetables in a separate pot. Turn the water down to a simmer, and add the lightly steamed vegetables with the steaming water.

5 tablespoons barley, rinsed
1 teaspoon sea salt, or to taste
Black pepper, to taste
⅓ cup dried split peas
Chopped parsley, for garnish

Add the barley, sea salt, black pepper, and soaked peas. Cover the pot and simmer for 1½ hours. Garnish with chopped parsley.

Per serving: Calories 215, Protein 2 g, Fat 3 g, Carbohydrates 46 g

Tomato Soup

Yield: 8 cups

Chop the tomatoes into small pieces (if you don't mind including the skins), or simply rub them over a grater to get the juice and pulp.

3 cups fresh tomatoes

Steam the onion, celery, and carrot until the onion is soft.

1 medium onion, chopped
2 stalks celery, chopped
1 carrot, grated

Add the oregano, basil, and tomatoes to the steamed vegetables, and simmer gently for 15 minutes. If you want a smooth, creamy texture, purée the soup in a blender or food mill.

¼ teaspoon oregano
1½ teaspoons basil

Add the hot stock and bring the soup to a boil. Simmer for 5 minutes. Season with the sea salt and cayenne pepper to taste. For a thicker soup, use only 2 or 3 cups of stock and reduce the seasonings accordingly.

1 quart hot vegetable stock
1½ teaspoons sea salt
Cayenne pepper, to taste

Per cup: Calories 24, Protein 1 g, Fat 0 g, Carbohydrates 5 g

Vegetable Gumbo

Yield: 8 to 9 cups

1 onion, chopped
3 cloves garlic, chopped
1 green pepper, diced
1½ cups sliced okra
2 cups diced tomatoes

Steam the onion, garlic, green pepper, okra, and tomatoes for 5 minutes, or until soft. Save the steaming water.

4 cups water
1 cup fresh corn
1 cup cooked lima beans
1 cup vegetable stock
1 teaspoon sea salt
¼ teaspoon allspice

Bring the 4 cups of water to a boil, add the steamed vegetables, steaming water, and the remaining ingredients. Simmer for 15 minutes.

½ cup cooked brown rice (optional)

Add cooked rice, if desired.

Per cup: Calories 66, Protein 3 g, Fat 0 g, Carbohydrates 13 g

Yellow Split Pea Soup

Yield: 3 servings

Crockpot Method: Place the soaked split peas in a crockpot, and add the 3 cups of water. Use the setting recommended by the manufacturer of your cooker for cooking split peas, and cook for 4 hours. One hour before serving, add the onion, carrot, marjoram, and thyme. Just before serving, add the sea salt, black pepper, and miso to taste.

Stovetop Method: Place the soaked split peas in a soup pot, and add the 3 cups of water. Bring to a boil, lower the heat, and simmer for 1 hour. Add the onion, carrot, marjoram, and thyme, and continue to cook for another ½ hour. Remove from the heat and add the sea salt, black pepper, and miso to taste.

1 cup yellow split peas, soaked overnight, rinsed, and drained
3 cups water
1 medium onion, finely chopped
1 carrot, chopped
1 teaspoon leaf marjoram, or ¼ teaspoon powdered marjoram
½ teaspoon thyme
Sea salt, to taste
Black pepper, to taste
1 tablespoon miso, or to taste

Per serving: Calories 229, Protein 13 g, Fat 0 g, Carbohydrates 42 g

Salads, Dressings, Sauces, and Dips

Salad Ingredients

There is no end to the possible combinations that could make up a delicious salad. Use the following lists to go beyond the traditional iceberg lettuce, tomatoes, and cucumbers, and explore flavor combinations that will bring more variety to your meals.

Greens:

Beet greens
Cabbage, green or
    red
Carrot tops
Celery & tops
Chicory
Chinese cabbage
Comfrey
Dandelion greens
Endive
Escarole
Green onions
Green peas, whole
    and edible pod
Lettuce (all types)
Mustard greens
Redwood sorrel
Romaine
Scallions
Spinach
Swiss chard
Turnip greens
Watercress

Herbs and Spices (fresh or dried):

Anise
Basil
Caraway
Celery seed
Chervil
Chive
Coriander
Cumin
Dill
Fennel
Flax
Ginger
Marjoram
Mint
Mustard
Oregano
Parsley
Poppy
Rosemary
Sage
Savory
Sesame
Tarragon
Thyme

Additional Suggestions:

Asparagus tips
Avocado
Beans, cooked
    (kidney or
    garbanzo)
Beets (grated or
    pickled)
Black olives
Broccoli
Carrots
Cauliflower
Cucumber
Dulse
Garlic
Kelp powder
Onions (all types)
Peppers, green or red
Radishes
Sauerkraut
Sprouts
Tofu
Tomato (all types)
Water chestnuts

Nuts & Seeds (whole or crushed):

Almonds
Pumpkin (hulled)
Soy nuts

Squash (hulled)
Sunflower (hulled)
Walnuts

Cole Slaw

Yield: 4 servings

Mix all the ingredients in a large bowl. Chill well before serving.

1 cup shredded green cabbage
1 cup shredded red cabbage
1 large carrot, shredded
⅛ cup grated onion
3 tablespoons toasted sesame oil
3 tablespoons Tofu Mayonnaise, p. 54, or Soy Yogurt, p. 60
2 tablespoons wheat-free tamari or sea salt
1 tablespoon celery seeds
1 tablespoon kelp powder
1½ teaspoons garlic powder
¼ teaspoon black pepper
1-2 tablespoons caraway seeds

Per serving: Calories 139, Protein 1 g, Fat 11 g, Carbohydrates 5 g

Cucumber Salad

Yield: 1 serving

⅓ cucumber
1 clove garlic, pressed
2 small green chilies, chopped
1 medium tomato, chopped into segments
3 tablespoons wheat-free tamari
2 tablespoons lemon juice
1 tablespoon ground roasted cashews

Chop the cucumber lengthwise into very fine matchsticks, and place in a bowl. Add the garlic and chilies to the cucumber. Mix in the tomato, tamari, and lemon juice. Add the ground cashews, combine gently, and serve.

Per serving: Calories 183, Protein 10 g, Fat 5 g, Carbohydrates 25 g

Fresh Spinach Salad

Yield: 2 servings

Thoroughly wash the spinach, tearing the larger leaves. Drain well. Add the mushrooms and green onions, and toss well. Sprinkle with tamari, if desired, then sprinkle each serving with sesame seeds.

2 cups spinach
½ cup sliced mushrooms
¼ cup chopped green onions
Sea salt, to taste (optional)
Sesame seeds, for garnish

Per serving: Calories 18, Protein 1 g, Fat 0 g, Carbohydrates 3 g

Greek Salad

Yield: 2 servings

1 large cucumber, sliced
1 large tomato, cut in wedges
1 cup crumbled extra-firm tofu
½ cup sliced black olives (Greek, if
    available)
½ small red onion, thinly sliced
Fresh spinach leaves
2 teaspoons dried mint (optional)

Combine the salad ingredients in a large bowl.

Dressing:
¼ cup olive oil
¼ teaspoon sea salt
3 tablespoons lemon juice
1 clove garlic, minced

Mix the dressing ingredients in a small bowl, and beat with a fork or whisk until well blended. Pour over the salad and toss.

Per serving: Calories 454, Protein 11 g, Carbohydrates 16 g

Missing Egg Salad

Yield: 4 servings

This versatile recipe can also double as a sandwich spread.

Combine all the ingredients, mix well, and chill.

3 cups tofu, crumbled
½ medium onion, chopped
2 stalks celery, chopped
¼ cup pickle relish
2 tablespoons lemon juice
1 tablespoon parsley
1 tablespoon mustard
2 teaspoons wheat-free tamari
1½ teaspoons garlic powder
1 teaspoon kelp
1 teaspoon paprika

Per serving: Calories 177, Protein 13 g, Fat 8 g, Carbohydrates 10 g

Potato Salad

Yield: 6 servings

6 medium potatoes

2 green onions, chopped
1 cup diced celery
½ cup shredded carrots
1 sprig parsley, chopped
1 cup diced red cabbage
1 cup Tofu Mayonnaise, p. 54
6-7 tablespoons olive oil
3-4 tablespoons white wine vinegar
Sea salt, to taste
1 whole clove garlic, crushed
　(optional)

Cut the potatoes into quarters, and steam in salt water until almost tender. Cool and cut into cubes.

Add the onion, celery, carrots, red cabbage, and parsley. Mix together with the remaining ingredients, and refrigerate for at least 1 hour.

Per serving: Calories 350, Protein 2 g, Fat 22 g, Carbohydrates 33 g

Szechuan Salad

Yield: 4 to 6 servings

Preheat the oven to 350°F. Mix the tamari and savory, and spread evenly over the thinly sliced tofu. Bake for 15 minutes on each side.

Slice the baked tofu into cubes, and combine with the remaining salad ingredients in a large bowl.

Mix the ingredients for the dressing, add to the salad, and toss.

Salad Ingredients:
2 tablespoons wheat-free tamari
1 teaspoon crushed savory
½ lb. tofu, thinly sliced

2 cups each shredded green and purple cabbage
½ carrot, sliced into thin circles
½ zucchini, thinly sliced
½ cup sprouts
6-8 (2-inch) bamboo shoots, thinly sliced
¼ bunch parsley or watercress, chopped

Dressing:
¼ cup safflower oil
1 tablespoon toasted sesame oil
½ cup apple cider vinegar
2 tablespoons grated gingerroot
2 tablespoons water
1 tablespoon wheat-free tamari
½ teaspoon black pepper, or to taste

Per serving: Calories 192, Protein 5 g, Fat 15 g, Carbohydrates 8 g

Tropical Fruit Salad

Yield: 4 servings

1 ripe banana
⅓ cup grated coconut
1 teaspoon liquid sweetener
4 tablespoons orange juice

1 banana, sliced
1 orange, divided into segments
1 cup papaya cubes
2 cups pineapple chunks
Other seasonal fruit (strawberries,
    grapes, etc.–optional)

Blend the whole ripe banana with the grated coconut, liquid sweetener, and orange juice.

Toss the fruit pieces together gently, and place in a hollowed-out pineapple shell. Top with the banana-coconut sauce, and serve.

Per serving: Calories 266, Protein 3 g, Fat 11 g, Carbohydrates 37 g

Salad Dressing Ingredients

Like a creative salad combination, a salad dressing can be just the beginning of a wonderful flavor adventure. Try out exotic vinegars or some of the miscellaneous ingredients listed below.

Oil:
Canola
Olive
Soybean
Toasted sesame

Vinegar:
Balsamic
Herbal
Rice wine

Lemon or lime juice

Herbs and Spices:
Basil
Cayenne
Cilantro
Herbamare
    seasoning blend
Marjoram
Oregano
Tarragon
Thyme

Miscellaneous:
Dijon mustard
Garlic
Ginger juice
Horseradish
Onion
Rice bran syrup
Shallots
Shiitake mushrooms
Tahini
Wheat-free tamari
Umeboshi plums
White miso

Garlic Tofu Dressing

Yield: 1 cup

½ cup crumbled tofu
2½ tablespoons lemon juice
2 tablespoons wheat-free tamari
2 tablespoons water
1 tablespoon finely chopped onion
1 tablespoon sesame, sunflower, or
    olive oil
2 teaspoons prepared mustard
½ teaspoon chopped dill weed
1 clove garlic, crushed

Combine all the ingredients in a blender, and blend until smooth. Store in the refrigerator.

Per tablespoon: Calories 17, Protein 1 g, Fat 1 g, Carbohydrates 0 g

French Dressing

Yield: 1½ cups

Thoroughly blend all the ingredients, and store in the refrigerator.

½ cup catsup
½ cup Tofu Mayonnaise, p. 54
¼ cup oil
2 tablespoons vinegar
1 tablespoon spice blend of your choice

Per tablespoon: Calories 48, Protein 0 g, Fat 2 g, Carbohydrates 5 g

Green Goddess Avocado Dressing

Yield: 2 cups

1 ripe avocado
1 small onion
½ cup oil
½ cup water
½ cup tofu
4 tablespoons fresh parsley, chopped
2 tablespoons apple cider vinegar
1 clove fresh garlic
¾ teaspoon sea salt
¼ teaspoon oregano

Thoroughly combine all the ingredients in a blender until smooth, and store in the refrigerator.

Per tablespoon: Calories 44, Protein 0 g, Fat 3 g, Carbohydrates 1 g

Herb Dressing

Yield: 1 cup

This is excellent with a tossed green salad.

Crush the garlic into a container, and add the remaining ingredients. Cover the container and shake well.

1 clove garlic
⅔ cup cold pressed oil
⅓ cup wine vinegar
¼ teaspoon basil
¼ teaspoon oregano
¼ teaspoon thyme
¼ teaspoon dill
¼ teaspoon dry mustard
¼ teaspoon kelp powder
¼ teaspoon paprika

Per tablespoon: Calories 79, Protein 0 g, Fat 9 g, Carbohydrates 0 g

Mustard

Yield: 1½ cups

This mustard recipe is English, using cider vinegar. Use red wine vinegar, or even wine, for a French variety, or champagne for French Dijon mustard. Chinese mustard can be created by using flat beer instead of vinegar. Plain water will make the taste even hotter, since vinegar tends to counteract the hotness.

2 tablespoons powdered mustard
2 tablespoons rice flour
½ teaspoon turmeric
½ teaspoon ground ginger

Mix the mustard, flour, and spices together.

1 cup cider vinegar
½ cup water
1 tablespoon liquid sweetener

Mix the vinegar, water, and liquid sweetener together. Combine the dry and liquid ingredients, and bring to a boil. Turn down the heat and let simmer for a few minutes. Pack into sterilized jars.

Per tablespoon: Calories 7, Protein 0 g, Fat 0 g, Carbohydrates 2 g

Russian Dressing

Yield: 1¼ cups

Combine all the ingredients and store in the refrigerator.

1 cup Tofu Mayonnaise, p. 54
¼ cup chili sauce
1 tablespoon horseradish
1 tablespoon finely chopped celery (optional)
1 tablespoon chopped green pepper

Per tablespoon: Calories 32, Protein 0 g, Fat 2 g, Carbohydrates 2 g

Soy Yogurt Dressing

Yield: 1 cup

1 cup Soy Yogurt, p. 60
2 teaspoons lemon juice
1 teaspoon dill

Combine by hand or in a blender, and store in the refrigerator.

Per tablespoon: Calories 19, Protein 1 g, Fat 0 g, Carbohydrates 1 g

Thousand Island Dressing

Yield: ⅔ cup

Thoroughly blend all the ingredients, and store in the refrigerator.

½ cup Tofu Mayonnaise, p. 54
2 tablespoons catsup
2 tablespoons cayenne
2 tablespoons liquid sweetener
2 tablespoons chopped sweet pickle
2 teaspoons chopped scallion or onion

Per tablespoon: Calories 48, Protein 0 g, Fat 2 g, Carbohydrates 5 g

Tofu Mayonnaise

Yield: 4¼ cups

3 cups crumbled tofu
1 cup oil
Juice of 1 lemon
1 teaspoon dill weed
1 teaspoon garlic powder
1 teaspoon liquid sweetener
1 teaspoon kelp
1 teaspoon sea salt
½ teaspoon mustard
¼ teaspoon white pepper

Combine all the ingredients in a blender until creamy and smooth; chill.

Per tablespoon: Calories 37, Protein 1 g, Fat 3 g, Carbohydrates 0 g

Tomato Catsup

Yield: 3 cups

Combine all the ingredients, adding more liquid sweetener if you prefer a very sweet catsup.

The purée can be made from scratch by cooking down tomatoes. Adding a tablespoon of arrowroot per cup of sauce will thicken it up to a paste and eliminate some of the cooking time needed. Keep refrigerated.

Chili Sauce: Double the amount of cinnamon, and add an equal amount of cayenne or other chili pepper. Keep refrigerated.

2 cups tomato purée
½ cup oil
¼ cup liquid sweetener
¼ cup apple cider vinegar
1 teaspoon sea salt
½ teaspoon cinnamon

Per tablespoon: Calories 30, Protein 0 g, Fat 2 g, Carbohydrates 2 g

Vinaigrette Dressing

Yield: 1¼ cups

½ cup olive oil
¼ cup apple cider vinegar
1 tablespoon chopped parsley
1 tablespoon chopped onion or
   chives
½ tablespoon lemon juice
¼ teaspoon dry mustard,
   or 1 teaspoon prepared Dijon
   mustard
1-3 cloves garlic, pressed
Dill, oregano, and basil, to taste
Tarragon, to taste (use sparingly)

Combine all the ingredients thoroughly.

Per tablespoon: Calories 49, Protein 0 g, Fat 5 g, Carbohydrates 0 g

Bechamel Sauce

Yield: 8 servings

This is truly an all-purpose sauce, great over steamed vegetables, cooked grains, pasta, or in casseroles. You can use it as the basis for the variations below or add your own favorite herbs, spices, and other seasoning combinations.

In a small saucepan, slowly heat the oil or margarine over low heat. Stir in the flour and cook over low heat for 3 or 4 minutes.

2 tablespoons oil or non-dairy margarine
3 tablespoons whole grain flour

In a separate pan, bring the soymilk to a boil. Reduce the heat to a simmer, then add the oil or margarine and whole grain flour mixture to the soymilk; stir with a whisk.

2½ cups soymilk

The sauce will begin to thicken after a few minutes. Add the onion and spices, and let it cook slowly for 10 to 15 minutes. Strain through a sieve to remove any lumps or large spice pieces.

½ onion, minced
1 bay leaf
Sea salt, white pepper, thyme, and nutmeg, to taste

Per serving: Calories 73, Protein 2 g, Fat 4 g, Carbohydrates 5 g

Tomato Bechamel Sauce: Add to the cooking Bechamel Sauce.

1 clove garlic, pressed
2 cups puréed vegetables
2 tablespoons wheat-free tamari, or to taste
½ cup tomato paste

Mornay Sauce: Gradually stir into 1 cup heated Bechamel Sauce.

½ cup grated soy cheese
1 teaspoon Dijon mustard
1 tablespoon oil or non-dairy margarine
1 tablespoon rice polishings

Chili Pepper Sauce

Yield: 2½ cups

2 cups tomato sauce
1 teaspoon ground red chili pepper
1 clove garlic, finely minced
Juice of 1 lemon
¼ cup finely minced onion
1 tablespoon grated horseradish

Combine all the ingredients, blend well, and store in the refrigerator.

Per ¼ cup: Calories 15, Protein 3 g, Fat 0 g, Carbohydrates 11 g

Low-Calorie Tofu Dips

One of the best ways to lose weight is to eat nutritious, tasty, low-calorie snacks between meals. This will help keep your blood sugar level from dropping, thus reducing mealtime binges. A tofu dip makes a perfect snack. Tofu is relatively low in calories—only 72 calories per 100 grams—and may be used in place of sour cream. Tofu dips are easy to prepare; just add a zesty sauce or juice and spices. Salt, wheat-free tamari, and miso will cause water retention; if you're watching your weight, go easy on these or avoid them completely.

You can make the dips listed below by adding the flavoring suggestions to taste while blending tofu:

Italian Dip: Use organic spaghetti sauce or tomato sauce. Add cayenne, garlic, oregano, basil, or bay leaf to taste. It may be thinned by blending with tomato juice, water, or lemon juice. It may be thickened with arrowroot. Serve hot or cold.

Pesto Dip: Blend fresh basil leaves with lemon juice and chopped or powdered garlic.

Mexican Dip: Use your favorite salsa. Add garlic, cayenne, or lemon to taste, if desired. You can make your own salsa by cutting up onions, tomatoes, jalapeño peppers, fresh cilantro, and fresh lime juice.

Indian Dip: Use curry sauce or curry powder and lemon juice. You may add turmeric, ginger, cayenne, fresh coriander (leaves or seeds), and cardamom to taste.

Szechuan Dip: Blend grated fresh gingerroot, garlic, hot red pepper or cayenne, tomato, bell pepper, green and white onions with lemon juice and water to taste.

Mustard Dip: Blend fresh tomatoes, steamed broccoli, Dijon, hot, or regular mustard, and lemon juice with water to taste. Beet or orange juice may be substituted for lemon.

Dill and Garlic Dip: Blend dill and minced garlic. Add lemon juice and water.

Herb Dip: Blend fresh or dried oregano, sorrel, marjoram, and caraway with lemon juice and water.

Onion Dip: Blend chopped white and/or green onions, garlic, cayenne, and lemon juice to taste.

Soy Cream Cheese

Soymilk

Let unsweetened soymilk set out unrefrigerated until it just thickens and slightly sours. Boil for 1 to 2 minutes in a saucepan until the curds separate from the whey. Pour into a colander lined with cheesecloth, and wring dry. Whip in a blender until you have a smooth paste. Add a little rich soymilk to soften and make a creamy consistency. Salt to taste.

Soy Yogurt

Yield: 1½ quarts

This yogurt is recommended for those who cannot tolerate dairy products.

6 cups soymilk
3 tablespoons fructose
1 package yogurt starter

Bring the soymilk almost, but not quite, to a boil. Cool to 110°F or until you can leave a clean finger in it for 10 seconds. Add the fructose and yogurt starter, and mix well. Pour into clean, sterilized glass jars, and cover with thick towels until the yogurt sets.

Per cup: Calories 112, Protein 6 g, Fat 5 g, Carbohydrates 12 g

Appetizers

Aunt Esther's Cheese Kugel

Yield: 6 to 8 servings

¼ cup oil
½ pint soy sour cream
1 lb. tofu
1 teaspoon cinnamon
8 oz. medium whole grain noodles,
  cooked and drained

Preheat the oven to 350°F. Add the oil, soy sour cream, tofu, and 1 teaspoon cinnamon to the noodles. Place in an oiled 9 x 15-inch pan.

Egg replacer equivalent to 3 eggs
½ cup fructose
2 cups soymilk or almond milk
1 teaspoon sea salt
1 teaspoon vanilla

Beat the egg replacer and add the fructose, soymilk or almond milk, sea salt, and vanilla. Pour over the noodles and refrigerate overnight.

1 teaspoon cinnamon, for topping
2 teaspoons fructose, for topping

Combine the remaining cinnamon and 2 teaspoons fructose, and sprinkle over the top. Bake for 1½ hours or until browned. Let the pudding stand ½ hour before serving.

Per serving: Calories 304, Protein 12 g, Fat 15 g, Carbohydrates 29 g

Hummus

Yield: 6 to 8 servings

Mix the sprouted chick-peas with the lemon juice and oil, and either mash or combine in a blender.

1-2 cups sprouted garbanzo beans (chick-peas)
Juice of 1 lemon
1 tablespoon olive oil

Add the remaining ingredients and blend to a creamy paste, adding water, if necessary. Garnish with additional paprika and parsley. Serve as a dip with pita bread.

Note: A quick dip, known in Middle Eastern countries as "taratoor," can be made by leaving out the garbanzo beans.

½ cup tahini
2-5 cloves garlic, mashed
1 tablespoon finely chopped parsley
¼ teaspoon paprika
¼ teaspoon cumin
¼ teaspoon coriander
¼ teaspoon cayenne
Sea salt, to taste

Per serving: Calories 175, Protein 5 g, Fat 10 g, Carbohydrates 15 g

Mint Chutney

Yield: ¼ cup

⅔ cup fresh mint leaves
¼ cup ground walnuts

1 teaspoon soy sour cream
½ teaspoon turmeric

Wash, dry, and mince the mint leaves. Mix them with the walnuts.

In a small cup, stir the soy sour cream and turmeric together, then blend with the mint and walnuts. Cover and allow to set for 30 minutes before serving.

Per tablespoon: Calories 50, Protein 1 g, Fat 4 g, Carbohydrates 2 g

Quinoa Tabouli

Yield: 3 servings

Quinoa is an ancient grain from the Andes now regaining popularity in this country. It is very high in protein and makes a delicious alternative to bulgur wheat. Be sure to rinse it before using to remove its bitter coating.

Black olives, carrot, cabbage, tofu, mushrooms, garlic, and cucumber slices would make delicious optional additions to this hot-weather salad.

Boil the 2 cups of water, lower to a simmer, and add the quinoa. Cover and cook 15 to 20 minutes until tender.

2 cups water
1 cup quinoa, well rinsed

Add the remaining ingredients to the quinoa, and mix well. Add more spices and lemon to taste; the salad should have a lemony flavor. Refrigerate.

1 cup lemon juice
1 cup finely chopped parsley
½ cup finely chopped onion and/or
    4 tablespoons finely chopped
    scallions
5 tablespoons olive oil
Herbamere seasoning, to taste
4 tablespoons finely chopped fresh
    mint, or 1½ tablespoons dried,
    crushed mint
Basil, dill, black pepper, thyme, and
    oregano, to taste

Per serving: Calories 437, Protein 9 g, Fat 23 g, Carbohydrates 44 g

Salsa

Yield: about 2 cups

2 large tomatoes, peeled, seeded,
    and chopped
1 onion, finely chopped
½-1 green jalapeño pepper, chopped
1 tablespoon chopped cilantro
1 tablespoon lime juice
1 clove garlic, crushed (optional)
Herbamare seasoning, to taste

Mix the ingredients in a bowl or grind in a blender. Adjust the seasonings to taste, and serve cold.

Per 2 tablespoons: Calories 9, Protein 0 g, Fat 0 g, Carbohydrates 2 g

Vegetarian Chopped Liver

Yield: 6-8 servings

Steam the onions and mushrooms until they are soft. Steam the tempeh for 20 minutes, then grate into a bowl. Combine all the ingredients in a food processor until smooth.

3 cups chopped onions
1 cup chopped mushrooms
½ lb. tempeh
1 cup finely grated carrots
¾ cup tahini
½ cup water
Black pepper, to taste
Garlic, to taste
Kelp, to taste
Wheat-free tamari, to taste

Per serving: Calories 245, Protein 10 g, Fat 13 g, Carbohydrates 19 g

Vegetable Quiche

Yield: 8 servings

Asparagus, bell pepper, or tomato may be added for variety.

Crust:
¾ cup whole grain flour
½ teaspoon sea salt
1 cup grated soy cheddar cheese

Stir together the flour and salt, then mix in the grated soy cheddar cheese and enough water to make a dough. Roll out the dough and place in an oiled pie pan or casserole dish.

Filling:
2 green onions, chopped
1½ cups chopped mushrooms
8 cups chopped spinach
1 teaspoon basil
1 teaspoon garlic powder

Preheat the oven to 375°F. Steam the onions, mushrooms, spinach, basil, and garlic until the onions are tender; drain off the liquid.

½ lb. soy cheese, sliced
3 cups crumbled tofu
1 tablespoon lemon juice
2 tablespoons tahini (optional)
Nutmeg, cayenne, and kelp, to taste

Cover the pie crust with the soy cheese slices. Blend the tofu, lemon juice, tahini, and spices until smooth. Mix in a bowl with the vegetables, and pour into the pie crust. Bake for 35 to 45 minutes.

Zucchini Quiche: Steam 2 diced zucchini along with the other vegetables.

Per serving: Calories 211, Protein 9 g, Fat 9 g, Carbohydrates 13 g

White Bean Pâté

Yield: 8 servings

Add the beans, onion, garlic, carrot, bay leaf, salt, and water to a crockpot or soup pot. Slow cook for 4 hours in a crockpot, or simmer on top of the stove for 45 minutes. Preheat the oven to 400°F. Oil a 2-quart casserole or pâté tureen.

1 cup navy beans or small white beans, soaked overnight, rinsed, and drained
1 small or medium onion, chopped
5 large cloves garlic, minced or pressed
⅔ cup finely grated carrot
1 large bay leaf
½-1 teaspoon sea salt, to taste
2 cups water

Put the cooked beans in a blender or food processor fitted with a steel blade. Add the egg replacer and lemon juice, and purée until smooth. Pour the bean purée into a mixing bowl. Add the bread crumbs, parsley, coriander, basil, and thyme, and mix everything together well. Adjust the sea salt and black pepper to taste.

Egg replacer equivalent to 2 eggs
2 tablespoons plus 1 teaspoon lemon juice
½ cup whole grain bread crumbs
¼ cup chopped fresh parsley
¼ teaspoon ground coriander
¼ teaspoon dried basil
¼ teaspoon dried thyme
Black pepper, to taste

Spoon the pâté mixture into the casserole or tureen, and cover tightly with a lid or foil. Bake for 50 to 60 minutes, or until the top begins to brown. Remove from the oven and serve warm or chilled. The flavors will develop more overnight. This dish freezes well.

Per serving: Calories 94, Protein 5 g, Fat 0 g, Carbohydrates 16 g

Main Dishes

Possible Burger Ingredients

Being a vegetarian opens up the possibilities for burgers way beyond beef. Try any of these cooked grains or beans (or a mixture of both). Add vegetables, and herbs and spices to taste. Use the binders listed below to help hold it all together. Add your favorite burger topping.

Grains (cooked and cooled):

Buckwheat
Millet
Rice, basmati or brown

Beans (cooked):

Black beans
Garbanzo beans
Lentils
Pinto beans
Split peas
Soybeans
Soy grits
Tempeh
Tofu

Nuts and Seeds:

Almonds
Almond butter
Caraway seeds
Sunflower or sesame seed meal
Tahini
Walnuts

Vegetables and Fruits:

Bell peppers, green or red
Broccoli
Carrots
Celery
Eggplant
Lemon juice
Jalapeño peppers
Jicama
Onions
Tomato sauce

Binder:

Almond butter
Tahini
Potatoes, steamed or baked, then mashed
Bread crumbs
Egg replacer
Oats
Olive oil
Whole grain flour

Herbs and Spices:

Basil
Cayenne
Cilantro
Coriander
Cumin
Curry powder
Dill weed
Dijon mustard
Dry mustard
Garam masala
Garlic
Ginger
Kelp
Marjoram
Mustard
Oregano
Parsley
Sage
Sea salt
Sorrel
Wheat-free tamari
Thyme
Turmeric

Toppings:

Catsup
Mustard
Sesame seeds
Salsa
Soy cheese
Wheat-free tamari

Eggplant Burgers

Yield: 8 burgers

Cut the eggplant into cubes, and steam until tender. Remove the eggplant from the steamer, and drain in a colander. Put in a mixing bowl or food processor, and add the beaten egg replacer and other ingredients. Allow to stand so the crumbs or wheat germ have softened and all the flavors have blended, about ½ hour.

Preheat the oven to 400°F. Sprinkle your hands with flour, and shape the mixture into burgers. Place on an oiled cookie sheet, and bake for 15 minutes on each side.

1 eggplant
Egg replacer equivalent to 2 eggs
½ cup whole grain bread crumbs
1 tablespoon rice flour
1 tablespoon soy flour
1 tablespoon oregano
1 tablespoon parsley
Garlic powder, to taste

Per burger: Calories 62, Protein 3 g, Fat 0 g, Carbohydrates 11 g

Grain Burgers

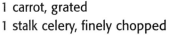

Yield: 10 to 12 burgers

1 carrot, grated
1 stalk celery, finely chopped
2 tablespoons minced fresh parsley

3 cups cooked grains
½ cup sesame or almond butter
1 tablespoon soy flour
Sea salt, to taste

Preheat the oven to 350°F. Steam the carrot, celery, and parsley until tender.

Mix all the ingredients together, and season to taste with sea salt. Adjust the amount of nut butter and soy flour, if necessary, to help the mixture hold together. Shape the mixture into patties. Bake for 20 minutes or until golden brown.

Per burger: Calories 141, Protein 6 g, Fat 6 g, Carbohydrates 17 g

Lentil Burgers

Yield: 8 burgers

Preheat the oven to 400°F. Mix all the ingredients well, and shape into patties. Place on an oiled cookie sheet, and bake for 15 minutes on a side. Serve plain or top with soy cheese or gravy.

2 cups cooked lentils

½ cup finely chopped onions

½ cup sunflower seeds (raw or toasted)

½ cup whole grain bread crumbs

¼ cup grated carrots

¼ cup finely chopped celery

2 teaspoons Herbamare seasoning

2 teaspoons thyme

Per burger: Calories 142, Protein 7 g, Fat 5 g, Carbohydrates 18 g

Nut Seed Burgers

Yield: 4 burgers

½ cup ground almonds
½ cup ground raw sunflower seeds
1 carrot, grated
1 stalk celery, finely chopped
½ cup finely chopped onion
Egg replacer equivalent to 1 egg
1 tablespoon cold pressed oil
1 teaspoon dill weed
1 teaspoon marjoram
Garlic powder, to taste
Black pepper, to taste.

Preheat the oven to 350°F. Grind the nuts in a coffee grinder or food processor, and chop the vegetables into small pieces. Mix all the ingredients together, and shape into burgers. Bake for 15 minutes on each side on an oiled cookie sheet.

Per burger: Calories 276, Protein 9 g, Fat 21 g, Carbohydrates 12 g

Tofu Burgers

Yield: 8 burgers

Preheat the oven to 350°F. Steam all the vegetables (including the parsley) until they are soft.

1 onion, finely chopped
1 cup finely chopped mushrooms
1 stalk celery, finely chopped
1 carrot, grated
2 tablespoons finely chopped fresh parsley

Combine the steamed vegetables with the remaining ingredients, and mix thoroughly. Add enough rolled oats to form a fairly stiff mixture which will hold together.

Form burgers, place on an oiled baking sheet, and bake 15 minutes on each side, or until browned. Serve with toasted bread or buns.

1 lb. tofu, mashed
1 cup whole grain bread crumbs
½ cup rolled oats (more as needed)
Egg replacer equivalent to 2 eggs
1 tablespoon olive oil
1 tablespoon prepared mustard
2 teaspoons cumin
½ teaspoon curry powder
½ teaspoon sea salt
¼ teaspoon black pepper, or to taste

Per burger: Calories 156, Protein 9 g, Fat 5 g, Carbohydrates 17 g

Savory Tempeh Burgers

Yield: 4 burgers

½ lb. tempeh, sliced

Marinade:
½ teaspoon grated fresh gingerroot
3 tablespoons water
¼ teaspoon dry mustard
2 tablespoons wheat-free tamari
1 tablespoon lemon juice
1-2 cloves garlic, or garlic powder, to taste
2 tablespoons apple cider vinegar or brown rice vinegar

Steam the tempeh for 20 minutes.

Mix the marinade ingredients and marinate the tempeh for ½ hour to several hours. Preheat the oven to 350°F, then bake the tempeh slices for 15 to 20 minutes.

Per burger: Calories 121, Protein 10 g, Fat 4 g, Carbohydrates 11 g

Soy Burgers

Yield: 8 burgers

Preheat the oven to 400°F. Mix all the ingredients well, shape into patties, and place on an oiled cookie sheet. Bake for about 15 minutes on a side.

1 cup cooked soybeans
1 cup cooked brown or basmati rice
1 cup tahini
Egg replacer equivalent to 2 eggs
⅓ cup whole grain flour
2 teaspoons wheat-free tamari
1 teaspoon garlic
1 teaspoon oregano
1 teaspoon dill
Herbamare seasoning, to taste

Per burger: Calories 266, Protein 11 g, Fat 15 g, Carbohydrates 20 g

Basic Brown Rice

Yield: 3 cups

Sea vegetables like kombu and wakame are a flavorful way to add both salt and nutritious minerals to your rice.

2 cups water
1 cup brown rice
1 teaspoon sea salt, 1 strand kombu, or several strands wakame

Bring the water to boil, and add the brown rice and sea salt or sea vegetable. Return to a boil, lower the heat to a gentle simmer, cover, and cook for 45 minutes.

Per cup: Calories 230, Protein 5 g, Fat 0 g, Carbohydrates 50 g

Basic Vegetable Pie

Yield: 8 servings

Line a 9-inch pie pan or baking dish with the crust.

9-inch crust of your choice

Steam the potato and carrot for 7 minutes; save the steaming water.

1 potato, finely diced
1 carrot, thinly sliced

Place all the vegetables and steaming water in a saucepan. Add the tofu, herbs, and spices. Cover and cook over low heat, stirring occasionally, until the vegetables are tender. Season to taste with the sea salt and cayenne pepper.

3 cups finely chopped mixed
   vegetables
½ green pepper, chopped
1 large tomato, chopped
¾ cup crumbled tofu
½ teaspoon basil
½ teaspoon oregano
½ teaspoon thyme
Sea salt and cayenne pepper, to taste

Preheat the oven to 350°F. Pour the vegetable mixture into the crust.

Top with the slices of cheese. Bake for 20 minutes or until the cheese is melted.

Soy cheese slices

Per serving: Calories 163, Protein 6 g, Fat 7 g, Carbohydrates 19 g

Bean Tostadas or Tacos

Yield: 6 to 8 servings

2 cups dried pinto or black beans, soaked overnight, rinsed, and drained
1 medium onion, chopped
Cayenne, cumin, and/or coriander, to taste
2 cloves garlic, chopped
1 bay leaf
6 cups water
Corn oil or other light, cold-pressed oil (optional)

Simmer the soaked beans with the onion and spices in 6 cups of water until the beans are soft, about 2 hours. Add the oil when the beans have finished cooking. (This will give the beans a refried flavor without actually heating the oil.) Mash the beans.

6-8 large corn tortillas or taco shells
2 cups chopped lettuce
1 carrot, grated
1 bell pepper, chopped
½ cucumber, chopped
1 cup sprouts
3 black olives, chopped
½ avocado, sliced
½ cup salsa

Steam the tortillas or heat them on a dry griddle or heavy pan; heat the taco shells in a warm oven or toaster oven. Place the chopped lettuce on top of the tortilla or taco shell. Then add the beans, carrot, bell pepper, cucumber, sprouts, olives, avocado, and salsa on top. Wrap the tortillas and/or arrange the filled tacos on plates.

Per serving: Calories 187, Protein 7 g, Fat 4 g, Carbohydrates 32 g

Brown Rice Almondine

Yield: 4 servings

Bring the water to a boil. Turn the heat down to a simmer, and add the rice and salt. Cook for 45 minutes. Add the oil and miso, and mix with the rice and almonds.

2½ cups water
1 cup brown rice
1 teaspoon sea salt
¼ cup oil
1 tablespoon miso
1 cup chopped or slivered almonds

Per serving: Calories 483, Protein 10 g, Fat 30 g, Carbohydrates 40 g

Cashew Rice with Peas

Yield: 2 servings

In a 1-quart saucepan, bring 2 cups of water to a boil, turn down to a simmer, and add the rice, peas, turmeric, tamari, and asafoetida, if using. Cover and cook on very low heat for about 20 minutes.

2 cups water
1 cup basmati rice
½ cup green peas
Pinch of turmeric
1 teaspoon wheat-free tamari
Pinch of asafoetida or hing (optional)

Stir in the cashew pieces, and serve.

½ cup roasted cashew pieces

Per serving: Calories 451, Protein 11 g, Fat 17 g, Carbohydrates 63 g

Chinese Mixed Vegetables

Pick one or more items from each group, steam or wok-fry (stir-fry) them in water, mix with a sauce, and serve with rice. You will have a delicious meal. The "crisp vegetables" should be steamed first, because they take longer to cook.

Crisp Vegetables:

Asparagus
Broccoli
Carrots
Cauliflower
Celery
Peas
Potatoes
Radishes
Turnips
Zucchini

Soft Vegetables:

Bok choy
Cabbage
Eggplant
Green beans
Mustard greens
Onions
Snow peas
Spinach
Swiss chard
Tomatoes

Chinese Vegetables:

Bamboo shoots (crisp)
Bean Sprouts
Shiitake Mushrooms
Water chestnuts (crisp)

Protein:

Almonds
Cashews
Tofu
Walnuts

Some Tasty Vegetable Combinations

Mushrooms with either:

Mustard greens and tofu
Snow peas and tofu
Cabbage, snow peas, and bamboo shoots

Sweet and Sour Vegetables:

Carrots
Celery
Tofu
String beans
Sweet and Sour Sauce, p. 86

Sweet and Sour Vegetables with Walnuts:

Bell peppers
Black mushrooms
Carrots
Sweet and Sour Sauce, p. 86
Tomatoes
Walnuts
Water chestnuts

Chow Mein:

1 lb. wheat-free noodles, cooked drained, and rinsed
1-2 cloves garlic, crushed
1 onion, thinly sliced
3-4 oz. cabbage, sliced into ¼-inch strips
4 large shiitake mushrooms, sliced into matchsticks
4 tablespoons Hoisin Sauce, p. 85
Cayenne and cherry juice to taste

Lo Han Mixed Vegetables:

Bamboo shoots
Broccoli
Cabbage
Celery
Eggplant
Garlic
Green beans
Wheat-free noodles
Onion
Tofu

Black Bean Sauce

Yield: 4 to 6 servings

Bring the water to a boil in a small saucepan. Stir in the remaining ingredients, and continue stirring until the sauce is smooth. Let simmer about 5 minutes.

¼ cup water
1 cup cooked black beans
¼ cup wheat-free tamari
2 large cloves garlic, pressed
¼ teaspoon sea salt
1 green onion, chopped
Grated fresh gingerroot, to taste
Black pepper, to taste

Per serving: Calories 56, Protein 4 g, Fat 0 g, Carbohydrates 10 g

Hoisin Sauce

Yield: ½ cup (8 servings)

Combine all the ingredients in a small bowl, and serve.

3 tablespoons dark miso
3 tablespoons brown rice vinegar
3 tablespoons brown rice syrup
3 tablespoons fructose
2½ teaspoons black pepper
2½ teaspoons garlic powder
1 teaspoon powdered ginger

Per serving: Calories 56, Protein 1 g, Fat 0 g, Carbohydrates 12 g

Sweet and Sour Sauce

Yield: 6 to 8 servings

3 tablespoons catsup or tomato paste
3 tablespoons apple cider vinegar
2-3 tablespoons pineapple, orange, or other citrus juice
2 tablespoons liquid sweetener
2 tablespoons wheat-free tamari
2 tablespoons cherry juice
¾ tablespoon arrowroot blended in 4 tablespoons water (optional)
Grated fresh gingerroot, to taste

Combine all the ingredients in a saucepan. Use the arrowroot if you want a thicker sauce. Simmer and stir until hot.

Per serving: Calories 34, Protein 1 g, Fat 0 g, Carbohydrates 8 g

Coconut Lemon Rice

Yield: 2 servings

Be sure to use organic citrus peel, as non-organic citrus has been sprayed with chemicals which remain on the rinds.

Bring 2 cups of water to a boil, and add the rice and sea salt. Cover and simmer for 45 minutes.

1 cup brown rice
½ teaspoon sea salt

Add the curry powder, coconut milk and/or coconut, and grated lemon peel, and serve.

1 teaspoon curry powder
½ cup medium-thick coconut milk, or
  ½ cup grated coconut
1 teaspoon grated organic lemon or
  lime peel

Per serving: Calories 408, Protein 7 g, Fat 13 g, Carbohydrates 65 g

Enchiladas

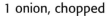

Yield: 12 servings

1 onion, chopped
3 cloves garlic, minced
1½ cups cooked kidney, soy, or pinto beans
1 cup sliced mushrooms
1 cup crumbled tofu
2 tablespoons sliced black olives
½ teaspoon oregano

Steam the onion and garlic until tender. Add the beans, mushrooms, tofu, black olives, and oregano, and cook for 5 minutes.

3 cups Enchilada Sauce (opposite page)
12 corn tortillas

Heat the enchilada sauce and dunk the tortillas into the sauce to soften. Preheat the oven to 350°F.

Optional Fillings (2 or 3 cups of filling is sufficient):
Grated soy cheese or grated soy cheese mixed with soy sour cream
Steamed, chopped spinach, mixed with soy sour cream or tofu cottage cheese
Guacamole
Refried pinto beans

Fill the tortillas with the tofu and bean mixture or any of the optional fillings, roll up, and set into a baking pan. Cover with the rest of the sauce, and bake for 30 minutes.

Per serving: Calories 141, Protein 6 g, Fat 2 g, Carbohydrates 24 g

Enchilada Sauce

Steam the Anaheim pepper and onion until soft. Add the steaming water and remaining ingredients (except the agar and green hot chilies), and combine in a blender. Dissolve the agar in a little hot water, and stir it into the blended sauce. Add the hot chilies and any additional spices to taste. Cook at a low simmer for 10 minutes. If the sauce seems too thick, stir in a little water.

1 large Anaheim pepper (mild green chili), diced

1 large onion, diced

1 cup of steaming water or hot vegetable broth

4 cups cooked, peeled, chopped tomatoes

3-4 cloves garlic, crushed

1 cup tomato juice or thinned tomato purée

½ teaspoon oregano

¼ teaspoon basil

¼ teaspoon cumin

2 tablespoons agar flakes

1-2 tablespoons diced green hot chilies, or to taste

Green Island Rice

Yield: 4 to 6 servings

1 cup chopped carrots
1 cup chopped cabbage
1 cup chopped spinach
1 cup chopped potatoes

Steam the carrots, cabbage, spinach, and potatoes until just tender.

2 cups water
1 cup brown or basmati rice

Bring the 2 cups of water to a boil, reduce the heat to a simmer, add the brown or basmati rice, and cook until tender (20 minutes for basmati, 40 minutes for brown).

1 teaspoon turmeric
1 teaspoon celery seed
1 teaspoon minced garlic
½ teaspoon Herbamare seasoning

Add the spices and vegetables, and combine well.

Per serving: Calories 162, Protein 4 g, Fat 0 g, Carbohydrates 35 g

Lasagne

Yield: 4 to 6 servings

Steam the spinach lightly.

6 cups chopped fresh spinach

Cook the lasagne noodles in boiling salted water until tender, then drain.

¾ lb. wheat-free lasagne noodles

Preheat the oven to 350°F. Toast the nuts or seeds in the oven, stirring frequently.

½ cup chopped almonds, sunflower seeds, or walnuts (optional)

Combine the tofu and soymilk or almond milk. Spread ¾ cup of the tomato sauce in the bottom of an 8 x 8-inch baking dish. Place ⅓ of the noodles on top. Cover with ⅓ of the spinach, ¼ of the nuts, 1 tablespoon rice polishings, ⅓ of the green olives, and a layer of the tofu mixture and soy cheese slices. Repeat the layers twice. Spread the last cup of sauce and the remaining nuts and cheeses on top. Bake for 40 minutes; let stand for 10 minutes before cutting.

¾ cup crumbled tofu
½ cup soymilk or almond milk
3 cups tomato sauce
¼ cup grated rice polishings
½ cup sliced green olives
12 thin slices soy mozzarella cheese

Per serving: Calories 359, Protein 19 g, Fat 13 g, Carbohydrates 37 g

Moussaka

Yield: 6 servings

1½ cups wheat-free macaroni

Cook the macaroni according to the package directions. Drain and set aside.

2 cloves garlic, crushed
1 onion, chopped
3 ripe tomatoes, cut into wedges
½ cup tomato purée
2½ teaspoons fresh oregano
Dash of nutmeg and cayenne pepper

Steam the garlic and onion. Add the fresh tomatoes and tomato purée, and cook for 10 minutes. Remove from the heat and stir in the macaroni and spices.

2 zucchini, sliced diagonally
2 small eggplants, cut into small chunks
1 cup oil
¼ cup whole grain flour
1 teaspoon sea salt
½ cup soymilk

Place the vegetables in a broiler pan. Brush with ¼ cup of the oil, and then sprinkle with 1 tablespoon of the flour and the salt. Broil on both sides until brown. Combine the remaining oil in a small saucepan with 3 tablespoons of the flour, and gradually add the soymilk to make a smooth sauce.

Grated soy cheese

Preheat the oven to 350°F. Oil a 2-quart casserole dish. Place a layer of vegetables on the bottom, then sprinkle with some of the grated cheese. Alternately fill the casserole with the remaining vegetables, soymilk sauce, tomato mixture, and cheese. Cover the top of the casserole with grated soy cheese, and bake for 1 hour. Serve warm.

Per serving: Calories 432, Protein 4 g, Fat 32 g, Carbohydrates 31 g

Noodles with Black Beans and Broccoli

Yield: 2 servings

Cook the rice noodles for 2 to 3 minutes in a large pot of boiling water; drain in a colander.

4 oz. rice noodles

Steam the broccoli for 7 to 10 minutes.

1 medium stalk broccoli, cut into florets

Heat the oil in a wok, add the garlic, and fry until golden brown. Combine the black beans, red chile, and sea salt, and stir well. Add the broccoli and vinegar, stir once, pour over the noodles, and serve.

2 teaspoons oil
1 clove garlic, finely chopped
1 cup cooked black beans
1 large fresh red chile, finely chopped
1 tablespoon sea salt
1 teaspoon rice vinegar

Per serving: Calories 454, Protein 13 g, Fat 15 g, Carbohydrates 69 g

Nori-Wrapped Sushi

Yield: 2 servings

These delicious Japanese delicacies are easy to make at home, especially if you have leftover cooked brown rice. You can find any unfamiliar Oriental ingredients in specialty food markets or health food stores.

1 cup cooked brown rice or sushi rice
1 tablespoon rice wine vinegar or
  other vinegar
Wheat-free tamari, to taste

Combine the brown rice and vinegar with the tamari.

2 sheets toasted nori

Place a sheet of toasted nori on a bamboo sushi mat or piece of waxed paper slightly larger than the nori. Spread ¼ cup of the rice evenly over the nori, leaving about ½ inch of nori uncovered on the top and bottom edges.

Possible sushi filling ingredients
  and combinations:
Bamboo shoots and shiitake
  mushrooms, cut into julienne
  strips
Chopped umeboshi plums
Spinach, cut into julienne strips,
  wheat-free tamari, and sesame
  seeds
Tofu and chives, cut into julienne
  strips, wheat-free tamari, and
  mustard

Place a row of julienned filling ingredients across the rice at the end nearest you.

Wet your fingers with a little water to prevent the nori from sticking to them. Starting at the side with the filling ingredients, roll the nori up over the filling, like a jelly roll. Use the mat or wax paper to press down on the nori and rice, and continue to roll the nori up.

Moisten the uncovered nori at the far end, and press the roll closed. Tamp in any loose rice on the ends of the roll.

Place the roll on a cutting board or plate. With a very sharp, lightly moistened knife, cut the roll cross-wise into 10 small discs. Arrange on a platter. The sushi may be garnished with a sprinkle of sesame salt or minced parsley. Serve with grated daikon radish, pickled ginger slices, or wasabi paste* mixed with tamari.

*Wasabi is Japanese horseradish; it has a distinctive "bite." A paste can be made by mixing wasabi powder with tepid water. Let stand for 10 minutes.

Cucumber, cut into julienne strips, and wasabi* (Japanese horseradish)

Pickles, cut into julienne strips

Cooked seaweed, cut into julienne strips

String beans and carrots, cut into julienne strips

Avocado and tofu, cut into julienne strips

Grated carrots, cabbage, and fresh gingerroot

Per serving: Calories 89, Protein 2 g, Fat 0 g, Carbohydrates 19 g

Pizza

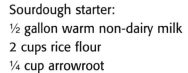

Sourdough Whole Grain Pizza Dough

Yield: 16 servings

Sourdough starter:
½ gallon warm non-dairy milk
2 cups rice flour
¼ cup arrowroot

Dough:
1½ cups warm water
2½ teaspoons sea salt
½ cup olive oil
2 cups sourdough starter
6½ cups brown rice flour

Make a sourdough starter by blending the warm non-dairy milk, 2 cups rice flour, and arrowroot. Let set at room temperature for 2 days.

Combine the warm water, sea salt, olive oil, and 2 cups of the sourdough starter. Add 2 cups of the whole grain flour, and let set for 20 minutes. Add and blend 4½ more cups of the flour. Gather the dough into a large ball on a floured board, and knead for 5-10 minutes. Place the dough in a bowl in a warm spot, and cover.

When the dough has doubled in bulk, divide it into 4 balls, and press the balls with the palm of your hand. Stretch them out by holding them up in the air and letting their weight stretch them. Use a rolling pin to work them into circles.

To make the sauce, simmer the chopped tomatoes in a saucepan until soft, then add the tomato paste, seasonings, and 1 cup water. Simmer for ½ hour.

Preheat the oven to 425°F. Place the dough onto lightly greased pizza pans, and form an edge to help keep the sauce inside the dough.

Remove the bay leaf from the sauce, and pour the sauce onto the dough. Sprinkle with the rice polishings and grated cheese, and top with mushrooms, green onions, olives, bell peppers, tomato slices, and zucchini, if you like. Bake for 30 to 45 minutes or until well browned. Let stand for ½ hour before serving.

Sauce:
2 cups chopped fresh tomatoes
1 (6-oz.) can tomato paste
½ onion, chopped
1 clove garlic, pressed
1 tablespoon oregano
1 teaspoon sea salt
½ teaspoon thyme
¼ teaspoon basil
¼ teaspoon cayenne, or to taste
1 bay leaf
1 cup water

½ lb. grated soy cheese
¼ cup rice polishings

Per serving: Calories 383, Protein 10 g, Fat 9 g, Carbohydrates 63 g

Possible Pizza Toppings

You can expand on the Pizza recipe on pp. 96, 97 by adding any of the following toppings or topping combinations:

Herbs, Spices, and Flavorings:

Basil
Chives
Cilantro
Fennel
Garlic
Ginger
Jalapeño peppers
Oregano
Pesto sauce
Parsley
Tarragon
Thyme

Vegetables:

Asparagus
Avocado
Broccoli
Red bell peppers
Red onions
Shiitake mushrooms
Spinach
Sun-dried tomatoes
Zucchini

Miscellaneous:

Black beans
Toasted sesame oil
Lime pickles
Pine nuts
Greek olives

Some Tasty Pizza Combinations

Italian-Style:

Fennel, basil, and sun-dried tomatoes

Mexican-Style:

Black beans, jalapeño peppers, and cilantro

Pesto Pizza:

Pesto sauce, pine nuts, and sun-dried tomatoes

Greek-Style:

Marinated tofu cubes, Greek olives, and spinach

Oriental-Style:

Shiitake mushrooms, ginger, and toasted sesame oil

Thai Pizza:

Asparagus, red bell peppers, shiitake mushrooms, garlic, ginger, cilantro, grated coconut, and wheta-free tamari
Top with tofu or black beans

Ratatouille

Yield: 4 servings

Preheat the oven to 350°F. Steam the vegetables until al dente.

2 large tomatoes, chopped
1 large onion, coarsely chopped
1 bell pepper, sliced
1 medium eggplant, peeled and cut into 1-inch cubes
1 medium zucchini, sliced into ½-inch rounds
2 cloves garlic, minced

Combine the vegetables and remaining ingredients, except the olive oil, and place in a casserole dish. Bake for 15 minutes.

2 cups tomato sauce
1-2 teaspoons basil
½ teaspoon oregano
Juice of ½ lemon
¼ teaspoon sea salt
⅛ teaspoon cayenne pepper

Mix in the olive oil after baking for additional flavor.

¼ cup olive oil (optional)

Per serving: Calories 119, Protein 3 g, Fat 0 g, Carbohydrates 25 g

Spaghetti with Marinara Sauce

Yield: 2 servings

This sauce derives its name from the wives of Italian mariners who would work all day preparing this sauce, anticipating their husbands' return.

Marinara Sauce:

1 eggplant or zucchini, cut into 1-inch squares
1 carrot, chopped
1 stalk celery, chopped
1 onion, chopped
1 bell pepper, chopped
1 (6-oz.) can tomato paste
4 cups coarsely chopped tomatoes, not drained
1 cup sliced mushrooms
1 tablespoon finely chopped garlic
1 tablespoon fresh oregano
1 tablespoon finely chopped fresh basil, or 1 teaspoon dried basil
1 bay leaf
1 teaspoon sea salt, or to taste
Cayenne pepper, to taste

Steam the eggplant or zucchini, carrot, and celery until tender. Add the onion and bell pepper, and continue steaming until the onion is soft; save the steaming water. Mix the steamed vegetables and steaming water with the tomato paste, chopped tomatoes, mushrooms, and spices. Turn the heat to low, and simmer uncovered, stirring occasionally, for 1 hour. The sauce should be thick and fairly smooth. Remove the bay leaf and season the sauce with sea salt and cayenne to taste.

8 oz. wheat-free spaghetti
½ teaspoon sea salt
¼ teaspoon olive oil

Bring 8 cups of water to a boil. Add the sea salt, spaghetti, and olive oil. Cook until a piece of spaghetti pressed against the side of the pan breaks easily and cleanly.

Per serving: Calories 433, Protein 16 g, Fat 1 g, Carbohydrates 87 g

Spicy Split Peas

Yield: 4 servings

Cook the soaked split peas in 4 cups of water for ½ hour or until tender.

1 cup dried yellow split peas, soaked overnight, rinsed, and drained

Lightly steam the onion, then mix with the turmeric and tomato sauce in a saucepan over low heat for 20 minutes. Mix together with the split peas, and add Herbamare to taste. Cook over medium heat for 10 to 15 minutes.

½ onion, diced
½ teaspoon turmeric
1 cup tomato sauce
Herbamare seasoning, to taste

Per serving: Calories 170, Protein 10 g, Fat 0 g, Carbohydrates 31 g

Spicy Vegetable Millet

Yield: 2 servings

2 cups water
1 cup millet

Bring the 2 cups of water to a boil, lower to a simmer, and add the millet. Simmer for 10 minutes.

2 green cabbage leaves, chopped
½ cup diced zucchini
¼ cup cashews
½ tablespoon oil
1 teaspoon cumin
1 teaspoon coriander
½ teaspoon black pepper
½ teaspoon mustard powder
Pinch of salt

Add the cabbage and zucchini, cashews, oil, and spices.

1 tablespoon fresh lemon juice

Stir in the lemon juice just before serving.

Per serving: Calories 552, Protein 15 g, Fat 16 g, Carbohydrates 88 g

Steamed Greens

Yield: 4 servings

Wash the greens thoroughly and cut up into the desired size. Steam the greens in ½ inch of water for 5 to 7 minutes, or until tender. Drain the greens in a colander, and season with black pepper and sea salt to taste.

2 lbs. collards, dandelion greens, mustard greens, or turnip greens
Black pepper and sea salt, to taste

Per serving: Calories 31, Protein 1 g, Fat 0 g, Carbohydrates 5 g

Stuffed Tomatoes

Yield: 2 servings

2 very large, ripe tomatoes

1 cup cooked long-grain brown rice
1 large Spanish onion, minced
¾ cup chopped walnuts
2 large cloves garlic, minced
Sea salt and cayenne pepper, to taste
1 cup boiling water

Preheat the oven to 350°F. Cut the tops off each tomato, and scoop out the pulp.

Mix the pulp with the remaining ingredients, and season well with sea salt and cayenne pepper to taste. Stuff the tomato shells with the mixture.

Arrange the tomatoes in a casserole, and pour the boiling water around them. Cover and bake for 25 minutes.

Per serving: Calories 530, Protein 32 g, Fat 11 g, Carbohydrates 46 g

Texas Chili with Beans

Yield: 8 to 10 servings

Adding fennel seeds while cooking this chili reduces the amount of gas you might get from eating the beans.

Crockpot Method: Place the soaked beans in a crockpot, and cover with water. Add the onions and garlic, and cook on low for 1 hour. Add the remaining ingredients, stir well, and cook 1 more hour, or until the beans are tender. Add more liquid during the cooking time, if necessary.

Stovetop Method: Place the soaked beans in a large soup pot. Cover with water, add the onions and garlic, and cook for 1 hour. Add the remaining ingredients, stir well, and cook for 1 more hour. Add more liquid if the chili begins to stick on the bottom.

1 lb. dried pinto beans, soaked overnight, rinsed, and drained
1 large onion, chopped
1 clove garlic, minced
1 (8-oz.) can tomato sauce, or 3 tomatoes, chopped
1 (6-oz.) can tomato paste
1 tablespoon fennel seeds
1-2 teaspoons chili powder or cayenne, or to taste
1 teaspoon oregano
1 teaspoon coriander
1 teaspoon cinnamon
1 teaspoon ground cumin
1 teaspoon paprika
1 teaspoon sea salt

Per serving: Calories 100, Protein 4 g, Fat 0 g, Carbohydrates 19 g

Tofu Stroganoff

Yield: 4 servings

This is also delicious made with tempeh steamed for 20 minutes.

1 lb. firm tofu

Drain the tofu to remove the excess water.

2 cups broccoli florets or green beans
10 mushrooms, sliced
1 medium onion, chopped
2 tablespoons garlic powder
¼ teaspoon white pepper
¼ teaspoon sea salt

Steam the broccoli florets or green beans until tender, then steam the mushrooms and onion until tender. Add the spices and steam for 2 minutes. Remove the mixture from the pan.

Slice the drained tofu in long strips, about 3 inches x ¾ inch x ½ inch. Steam the tofu until heated through, and add to the mushroom mixture.

1 cup soy sour cream
¼ cup wheat-free tamari
1-2 tablespoons cooking sherry or
   cherry juice

Combine the soy sour cream, tamari, and cooking sherry in a saucepan. Cook for a few minutes to blend together the flavors. If the sauce is too thick, add more sour cream. Adjust the amount of cooking sherry to your own taste. Serve the tofu over wheat-free, whole grain noodles or wild rice, and top with the cream sauce.

Per serving: Calories 231, Protein 14 g, Fat 11 g, Carbohydrates 17 g

Vegetable Brown Rice

Yield: 4 servings

Bring 2 cups of water to a boil, add the brown rice, and let simmer for 45 minutes or until all of the water is absorbed.

2 cups water
1 cup brown rice

While the rice is cooking, steam the vegetables.

1 small onion, chopped
1 scallion, chopped
½ cup green peas
½ cup bamboo shoots
4 shiitake mushrooms, chopped
½ celery stalk, sliced
1 slice fresh gingerroot, grated

Save the steaming water and stir in the sea salt, garlic, black pepper, and sherry to make a sauce.

½ tablespoon sea salt
1 clove garlic, minced
Black pepper, to taste
1 tablespoon sherry or cherry juice

Place the cooked rice in a bowl. Stir the sauce and vegetables into the rice, and serve hot.

Per serving: Calories 209, Protein 6 g, Fat 0 g, Carbohydrates 43 g

Vegetarian Shepherd's Pie

Yield: 6 servings

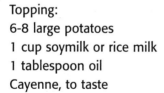

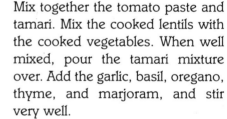

1 cup dried brown or green lentils
4 cups water

Rinse the lentils thoroughly and soak for 1 hour. Bring 4 cups of water to a boil, add the lentils, and reduce the heat to a low simmer. Cook for 1 hour.

2 cups cauliflower or broccoli florets
1 large green pepper, chopped
1 large onion, chopped
1 large carrot, thinly sliced

Steam the florets and green pepper for a few minutes until the florets begin to soften; then add the onion and carrot.

⅓ cup tomato paste
⅓ cup wheat-free tamari
Chopped garlic, to taste
½ teaspoon basil
¼ teaspoon oregano
¼ teaspoon thyme
¼ teaspoon marjoram

Mix together the tomato paste and tamari. Mix the cooked lentils with the cooked vegetables. When well mixed, pour the tamari mixture over. Add the garlic, basil, oregano, thyme, and marjoram, and stir very well.

Topping:
6-8 large potatoes
1 cup soymilk or rice milk
1 tablespoon oil
Cayenne, to taste

To make the topping, steam and mash the potatoes. Whip with the soymilk or rice milk until creamy. Add the oil and cayenne to taste.

Preheat the oven to 350°F.

Mix all the ingredients for the crust together well. Spread the mixture in an oiled pie pan or 1-quart casserole dish.

Millet Crust:
1½ cups cooked millet
¾ teaspoon sea salt
2 tablespoons sesame seeds

Fill with the vegetable mixture. Spread the mashed potato mixture over the vegetables, and sprinkle the grated soy cheese on top. Bake for 20 to 25 minutes, then place the pan under the broiler for a few minutes in order to brown the potatoes. Serve with baked beans.

½ cup grated soy cheese

Per serving: Calories 491, Protein 22 g, Fat 8 g, Carbohydrates 81 g

Vegetarian Sukiyaki

Yield: 6 servings

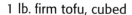

1 lb. firm tofu, cubed
1 carrot
5 oz. bamboo shoots
5 oz. water chestnuts
1 Bermuda onion, or 1 stalk green
   onion, chopped
1 stalk celery (optional)
¼ head cabbage or fresh spinach
   (2 cups)
6 pieces mochi (pressed, cooked
   sweet rice cakes, optional)
2 cups bean sprouts
10 fresh shiitake mushrooms
4 inches daikon radish, cut into
   ½-inch rounds

Thinly slice the vegetables diagonally. Steam-fry in a wok with water, or steam the vegetables 5 to 10 minutes.

Sauce:
½ cup water or mirin (Japanese
   sweet rice wine)
½ cup wheat-free tamari
1 teaspoon fructose
¼-½ teaspoon powdered ginger, or to
   taste
1 clove garlic, crushed
Cooked brown rice or yam noodles
   (optional)
Shichimi, to taste (a blend of 7 spices
   used to garnish Oriental rice and
   noodle dishes)

To make the sauce, bring the water or mirin to a boil, add the tamari, fructose, ginger, and garlic, and simmer for 5 minutes. Mix with the steamed vegetables. Serve with brown rice or yam noodles, and top with shichimi, to taste.

Per serving: Calories 152, Protein 10 g, Fat 3 g, Carbohydrates 19 g

Bread

Banana Bread

Yield: 8 servings

⅓ cup liquid sweetener
½ cup oil
3 medium ripe bananas, mashed
1 teaspoon vanilla
Egg replacer equivalent to 2 eggs

Preheat the oven to 350°F. Cream the liquid sweetener and oil, and stir in the bananas, vanilla, and egg replacer.

1½ cups whole grain flour
2 teaspoons baking powder
½ teaspoon sea salt
½ teaspoon cinnamon
½ cup chopped nuts (optional)

Combine the remaining ingredients and stir together with the banana mixture until just mixed.

Bake in an oiled 5 x 9-inch bread pan for approximately 1 hour or until golden brown. Test the center by inserting a toothpick in the bread; when the toothpick comes out clean, the bread is done.

Per serving: Calories 326, Protein 4 g, Fat 13 g, Carbohydrates 45 g

Basic Muffins

Yield: 12 muffins

Preheat the oven to 400°F. Sift the dry ingredients, then add the liquid ingredients all at once. Stir just to moisten the dry ingredients; the batter should be lumpy. Fill oiled muffin tins only two-thirds full, and bake for 20 to 25 minutes. Serve hot.

Dry Ingredients:
2 cups unsifted whole grain flour
2 teaspoons baking powder
2 tablespoons fructose
½ teaspoon sea salt

Liquid Ingredients:
¼ cup oil
1½ cups cold non-dairy milk
Egg replacer equivalent to 1 egg, beaten

Per muffin: Calories 166, Protein 3 g, Fat 5 g, Carbohydrates 25 g

Bran Muffins

Yield: 12 muffins

Preheat the oven to 400°F. Cream the oil and fructose. Dissolve the baking soda in the non-dairy milk, and add to the oil mixture. Stir in the remaining ingredients. Spoon into oiled muffin pans, and bake for 20 minutes. Let the muffins cool in the pans for 5 minutes before removing, as these muffins are exceptionally light.

1 cup oil or non-dairy margarine
¼ cup fructose
1 teaspoon baking soda
1 cup non-dairy milk
2 cups oat bran flakes
½ cup rice flour
½ cup raisins
Egg replacer equivalent to 1 egg

Per muffin: Calories 260, Protein 3 g, Fat 19 g, Carbohydrates 21 g

Bread Sticks

Yield: 10 sticks

1 pkg. active dry yeast (scant
tablespoon)
1¼ cups lukewarm water

3 cups whole grain flour
6 tablespoons oil or non-dairy
margarine
1-2 teaspoons sea salt

Egg replacer equivalent to 1 egg yolk
Additional salt, for topping
Caraway seeds, for topping

Combine the yeast and warm water, and let set until foamy, about 10 minutes.

Add the flour, oil and 1 to 2 teaspoons salt, and knead until the dough is no longer sticky on the surface. (You might have to add more flour or water to achieve the right consistency.) Let the dough set in a warm place for 20 to 30 minutes, then divide into 10 pieces.

Roll each piece into an 8-inch bread stick. Place the sticks on an oiled baking sheet. Brush with egg replacer and sprinkle on some salt and caraway seeds. Set in a warm place to rise for 20 to 30 minutes, then bake for 20 minutes at 400°F.

Per stick: Calories 262, Protein 4 g, Fat 9 g, Carbohydrates 41 g

Cornbread

Yield: 4 to 6 servings

Preheat the oven to 425°F. Mix the dry ingredients in a bowl.

Dry Ingredients:
1 cup cornmeal
1 cup barley flour
2 teaspoons baking powder
½ teaspoon baking soda
½ teaspoon sea salt

In a separate bowl, combine the non-dairy milk and vinegar, stir well, then add the rest of the liquid ingredients. Combine the dry and liquid mixtures, and mix well. Pour into an oiled and floured 9 x 9-inch baking pan, and bake for 20 minutes. Cut into squares and serve.

Liquid Ingredients:
1 cup non-dairy milk
1 tablespoon vinegar
¼ cup liquid sweetener
3 tablespoons oil or melted non-dairy margarine
Egg replacer equivalent to 1 egg

Per serving: Calories 329, Protein 7 g, Fat 9 g, Carbohydrates 53 g

Russian Black Bread

Yield: 1 loaf (12 slices)

The secret to Russian black bread is in using bread crumbs for some of the flour. You can save your crusts or stale pieces of bread or buy a loaf of dark bread, let it go stale, and make crumbs. To quicken the drying process, crumble the bread and toast it in the oven. Use these crumbs for the first batch of black bread. Then save the ends or stale pieces of the black bread that you have made, and make those into crumbs. Each subsequent loaf will be darker.

1 pkg. active dry yeast (scant tablespoon)
¾ cup lukewarm grain coffee (Pero, Roastaroma, etc.)
1 teaspoon fructose

Mix the yeast with the lukewarm grain coffee and fructose and let set.

⅓ cup molasses
¼ cup apple cider vinegar

In a saucepan, combine the molasses with the vinegar, and bring it to a boil.

¼ cup oil or non-dairy margarine
¼ cup carob powder

Turn off the heat and add the oil and carob. Let the mixture stand until lukewarm.

3 cups rye flour
1 cup whole grain bread crumbs or barley flour
2 teaspoons sea salt
2 tablespoons caraway seeds
1 teaspoon crushed fennel seeds
2 teaspoons onion powder
½ teaspoon grated fresh gingerroot, or 1 teaspoon powdered ginger

Stir in the yeast mixture, and add the rye flour, bread crumbs, sea salt, caraway seeds, fennel seeds, onion powder, and ginger. Stir until smooth, then place the dough on a lightly floured surface, and knead until smooth and shiny. Place the dough in a large, oiled bowl, cover with a towel, and let stand in a warm place for about 2 hours, or until doubled in bulk.

Knead the dough again for about 10 minutes, shape into a round loaf, and place on an oiled baking sheet. Cover with a towel and let rise again for about 1 hour, or until doubled in size.

Preheat the oven to 375°F. Bake for about 25 minutes, or until brown and the loaf sounds hollow when tapped with your finger. Cool on a rack.

Per slice: Calories 213, Protein 4 g, Fat 5 g, Carbohydrates 37 g

Whole Grain Bread

Yield: 3 large or 6 small loaves (30 slices)

2 pkgs. active dry yeast (scant 2 tablespoons)
1¼ cups lukewarm water
3 tablespoons liquid sweetener
1½ cups non-dairy milk
3 tablespoons oil
1 tablespoon salt

8-10 cups whole grain flour
1 cup rolled oats

Egg replacer equivalent to 1 egg yolk
Sesame seeds, for topping (optional)

(For a variation, add sunflower seeds or sesame seeds to the mixture when adding the flour.)

Dissolve the yeast in the water, and add 1 tablespoon of the liquid sweetener. Scald the non-dairy milk and add the oil, remaining liquid sweetener, and salt. Let the mixture cool to lukewarm, then add to the yeast mixture.

Gradually add the whole grain flour and oats, beating well. Turn out onto a lightly floured board, and knead until smooth and elastic. Place in a large, well-oiled bowl. Cover with a damp cloth or towel, and set in a warm place for about 1½ hours, or until the dough doubles in bulk.

Turn out onto the floured board. Punch down and knead again. Divide the dough into 3 equal loaves. Place in oiled loaf pans, brush with egg replacer, and sprinkle with sesame seeds, if desired. Cover with a damp cloth, and set in a warm place to rise again until almost double in bulk. Preheat the oven to 350°F.

Bake the loaves for about 1 hour, or until the loaves sound hollow when tapped on the bottom.

Per slice: Calories 221, Protein 5 g, Fat 2 g, Carbohydrates 46 g

Desserts

Candy Basics

The ingredients below can be combined in an almost unlimited number of ways to make healthful, nourishing candies. Select ingredients from both the dry and moist categories, then add additions and flavorings, if you like. Mix and press into square pans, then chill and cut into squares. The mixtures can also be shaped into balls and rolled in any of the dry ingredients listed below, wrapped individually in waxed paper, and chilled.

Moist:

Applesauce

Bananas

Black cherry or apple concentrate

Brown rice syrup

Fruit purée

Maple syrup

Molasses

Nut butter

Oil

Peanut butter

Pumpkin purée

Royal jelly

Tahini

Dry:

Bee pollen

Brewer's yeast

Brown rice flour

Carob powder

Chia seeds

Coconut, unsweetened, shredded, and finely ground

Cornmeal

Flax, ground

Graham cracker crumbs

Nuts, raw or toasted, and finely ground

Rice polishings

Rose hip powder

Sesame seeds

Sunflower seeds, whole or finely ground

Wheat germ, raw or toasted

Additions:

Apples

Apricots

Dates

Dried fruit, chopped and soaked

Figs

Prunes

Raisins

Flavorings:

Anise

Cardamom

Cinnamon

Date sugar

Extracts (vanilla, almond, etc.)

Ginger

Grated organic citrus rind

Juices

Licorice

Nutmeg

Raisin or date soaking water

Energy Boosters

Yield: 32 balls

Mix the ingredients and knead with your hands until stiff; form into balls. Keep refrigerated.

1 cup protein powder (such as soy isolate, etc.)

Cinnamon, nutmeg, cardamom, to taste

1 cup rice polishings

Chia seeds (optional)

1 cup soaked dried fruit

1 cup grated coconut (optional)

1 cup soaking water from the soaked dried fruit, or fruit juice

Per ball: Calories 47, Protein 4 g, Fat 0 g, Carbohydrates 7 g

Carob Tofu Creme Pie

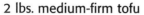

Yield: 8 servings

2 lbs. medium-firm tofu
½ cup safflower oil
⅓ cup liquid sweetener
⅔ cup roasted carob powder
2 teaspoons arrowroot
¼ teaspoon sea salt
½ teaspoon cinnamon
2 teaspoons vanilla

Preheat the oven to 350°F. In a large mixing bowl, mash the tofu and mix with the oil, liquid sweetener, carob, arrowroot, salt, cinnamon, and vanilla.

2 teaspoons grain coffee powder
  (Pero, Roastaroma, etc.)
⅔ cup hot water

Dissolve the grain coffee in the hot water, and mix with the tofu mixture. Combine in a blender until smooth—it's easier to do this in 2 batches.

1 unbaked 9-inch pie crust

Pour into an unbaked 9-inch pie crust, and bake for 35 minutes, or until the crust is done and the filling has set.

Per serving: Calories 398, Protein 10 g, Fat 25 g, Carbohydrates 31 g

Dairy-Free Tofu Cheesecake

Yield: 6 servings

Heat the soymilk and agar in a saucepan until boiling. Reduce the heat and simmer for 2 minutes.

1 cup soymilk
3 tablespoons agar flakes

Place the tofu, vanilla, lemon juice, lemon rind, and sweetener into a blender. Add the hot agar mixture, and blend until smooth.

1½ cups crumbled tofu
1 tablespoon vanilla
¼ cup lemon juice
1 tablespoon finely grated organic lemon rind
½ cup fructose

Add the carob powder, if desired. Pour the filling into a pie crust, and chill until firm. Top with your favorite fruit.

1 tablespoon carob powder (optional)
1 prepared 8- to 9-inch pie crust

Per serving: Calories 302, Protein 7 g, Fat 13 g, Carbohydrates 38 g

Uncooked Tofu Cheesecake

Yield: 10 servings

Crust:

1 cup granola

1 cup toasted slivered almonds

3 tablespoons oil or non-dairy margarine

¾ cup toasted shredded coconut

Mix the crust ingredients and press into the bottom of a 10-inch springform pan.

Filling:

2 lbs. medium-firm tofu

1 tablespoon carob powder

1 teaspoon vanilla

¼ teaspoon cinnamon

¾ cup fructose or brown rice syrup

1 tablespoon tahini

Combine the filling ingredients in a food processor or blender until smooth, then spoon onto the crust. Top with fruit or fruit sauce, if desired. Chill until set and serve.

Per serving: Calories 424, Protein 10 g, Fat 26 g, Carbohydrates 36 g

Whole Grain Pie Crust

Yield: 8 servings (2 crusts)

Here's a foolproof recipe for delicious, flaky pie crust. To get good results, be sure to use chilled oil and ice water.

Mix the flours and salt in a bowl. Add the oil and mix well with a fork or your hands to distribute evenly; the mixture will be lumpy. Add the ice water all at once, and mix quickly until the dough forms a ball. Divide into 2 balls and roll out between two layers of waxed paper, using short, light strokes at first. Peel off the top layer of waxed paper, invert over a pie tin, and peel off the other layer of paper. Trim the edges of the crust.

1½ cups barley flour
¾ cup oat flour
½ teaspoon sea salt
½ cup chilled safflower or canola oil
½ cup ice water

Per serving: Calories 229, Protein 4 g, Fat 14 g, Carbohydrates 21 g

Pumpkin-Tofu Pie

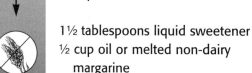

Yield: 8 servings

Crust:
¼ cup oatmeal
¾ cup coconut
¼ cup sesame seeds
½ cup oat flour

1½ tablespoons liquid sweetener
½ cup oil or melted non-dairy
    margarine

Filling:
3¼ cups mashed pumpkin
½ lb. tofu
1 cup soymilk
½ cup fructose
¼ cup arrowroot
¼ cup cashew butter
1½ tablespoons molasses
1 tablespoon vanilla
1 tablespoon cinnamon
1½ teaspoon powdered ginger
1 teaspoon nutmeg
½ teaspoon sea salt
¼ teaspoon cloves

To make the crust, toast the oatmeal, coconut, and sesame seeds in a large skillet until just starting to brown. Combine in a bowl with the oat flour.

Combine the liquid sweetener and oil, and add to the dry ingredients. Mix well and press into the bottom of a 9-inch pie pan.

Preheat the oven to 425°F.

Blend the filling ingredients in a food processor until smooth, or combine in a mixing bowl and blend in a blender in several batches.

Pour the filling into the pie shell, and bake for 15 minutes, then lower the temperature to 350°F, and bake for 45 minutes. The pie will firm up when cooled.

Per serving: Calories 305, Protein 8 g, Fat 33 g, Carbohydrates 43 g

Sweet Potato Pie

Yield: 8 servings

Steam the sweet potatoes until tender, then peel and mash.

3 large sweet potatoes

Preheat the oven to 350°F. Place the oil in the hot soymilk, and add to the sweet potatoes. Beat until soft and creamy.

3 tablespoons oil or non-dairy margarine
½ cup hot soymilk

Add the beaten egg replacer, fructose, sea salt, vanilla, and nutmeg to the sweet potato mixture, and mix well. Pour the filling into the crust, and bake for 30 minutes.

Egg replacer equivalent to 2 eggs, lightly beaten
½ cup fructose
½ teaspoon sea salt
½ teaspoon vanilla
¼ teaspoon nutmeg

1 unbaked pie crust

Per serving: Calories 317, Protein 4 g, Fat 12 g, Carbohydrates 46 g

Tofu Whipped Cream

Yield: 8 servings

Combine all the ingredients in a blender until smooth.

¾ lb. soft tofu (1½ cups)
3 tablespoons sweetener of your choice
Dash sea salt
1 tablespoon vanilla

Per serving: Calories 50, Protein 3 g, Fat 1 g, Carbohydrates 13 g

Almond Cookies

Yield: 1 dozen cookies

2 tablespoons cold-pressed almond oil
¼ teaspoon sesame oil

Preheat the oven to 350°F. Mix the oils together.

1 cup rice flour
1 teaspoon baking powder
½ teaspoon sea salt
Egg replacer equivalent to 1 egg
⅓ cup finely chopped almonds
1 teaspoon almond extract

Sift the flour, baking powder, and salt together. Add the oils and the egg replacer, and mix well. Add half the almonds and the extract (save ½ of the almonds for topping). Form the dough into 1-inch balls. Top each ball with some almonds, and bake on a nonstick cookie sheet for 20 minutes.

Per cookie: Calories 95, Protein 2 g, Fat 4 g, Carbohydrates 12 g

Almond Oat Cookies

Yield: 1 dozen cookies

1½ cups oat flour
½ teaspoon baking powder
⅛ teaspoon Herbamare seasoning
¼ teaspoon cinnamon

Preheat the oven to 350°F. Mix the flour, baking powder, Herbamare, and cinnamon.

½ cup almond butter
¼ teaspoon almond extract
4 tablespoons brown rice syrup
1 tablespoon oil
Almond slivers

In a separate bowl, blend the almond butter, extract, syrup, and oil. Combine the two mixtures well. Spoon onto a nonstick cookie sheet, top with almond slivers, and bake for 10 to 15 minutes.

Per cookie: Calories 145, Protein 3 g, Fat 8 g, Carbohydrates 15 g

Carob Chip Cookies

Yield: 3 dozen cookies

Preheat the oven to 350°F. Mix the flour, baking powder, and Herbamare in a mixing bowl, and set aside.

3½ cups rice flour
1½ teaspoons baking powder
¼ teaspoon Herbamare seasoning

In another bowl, whip together the fructose, margarine, egg replacer, and vanilla. Pour this mixture into the dry ingredients.

1½ cups fructose
1½ cups non-dairy margarine
Egg replacer equivalent to 2 eggs
½ teaspoon vanilla

After the mixture is fully blended, add the carob chips, and coconut and walnuts, if using. Spoon onto a nonstick cookie sheet, and bake for 10 to 15 minutes.

2 cups carob chips
Coconut (optional)
Walnuts (optional)

Per cookie: Calories 198, Protein 2 g, Fat 9 g, Carbohydrates 27 g

Coconut Cookies

Yield: 2 dozen cookies

1 cup brown rice flour
¾ cup barley flour
½ cup oat bran
½ teaspoon baking powder

½ cup barley malt or brown rice syrup
½ cup non-dairy margarine
¾ teaspoon vanilla

½ cup shredded coconut

Preheat the oven to 350°F. Mix the flours, bran, and baking powder.

In a separate bowl, blend together the barley malt or brown rice syrup, margarine, and vanilla. Combine the wet and dry ingredients, and add the shredded coconut. Drop by tablespoonfuls onto a nonstick cookie sheet, and bake for 10 to 15 minutes.

Per cookie: Calories 118, Protein 1 g, Fat 8 g, Carbohydrates 10 g

Ginger Snaps

Yield: 2 dozen cookies

Preheat the oven to 350°F. Mix the dry ingredients well.

Dry Ingredients:
1 cup rice flour
1 cup tapioca flour
1 teaspoon baking powder
1 teaspoon cinnamon
½ teaspoon powdered ginger
½ teaspoon Herbamare seasoning
¼ teaspoon ground cloves

In a separate bowl, cream the oil and brown rice syrup together, and add to the dry ingredients. Mix in the shredded coconut. Spoon onto a nonstick cookie sheet, and bake for 10 to 15 minutes.

½ cup oil or non-dairy margarine
½ cup brown rice syrup
½ cup shredded coconut

Per cookie: Calories 136, Protein 1 g, Fat 6 g, Carbohydrates 17 g

Oatmeal Cookies

Yield: 2½ dozen cookies

1½ cups oat flour
3 cups oats
1 teaspoon baking powder
1 teaspoon cinnamon
½ teaspoon powdered ginger
¼ teaspoon nutmeg

¼ cup non-dairy milk
1¼ cups non-dairy margarine
½ cup fructose or brown rice syrup
Egg replacer equivalent to 1 egg
1 teaspoon vanilla

Preheat the oven to 350°F. Mix together the flour, oats, baking powder, and spices.

In a separate bowl, blend the non-dairy milk, margarine, fructose or syrup, egg replacer, and vanilla. Combine both mixtures. Spoon onto a nonstick cookie sheet, and bake for 10 to 15 minutes.

Per cookie: Calories 137, Protein 2 g, Fat 8 g, Carbohydrates 13 g

Rice Flour Cookies

Yield: 2 dozen cookies

Preheat the oven to 350°F. Blend the flours, baking powder, Herbamare, and ground almonds.

1 cup brown rice flour
1 cup tapioca flour
½ teaspoon baking powder
½ teaspoon Herbamare seasoning
½ cup ground almonds

In a separate bowl, mix together the fructose or syrup, margarine, egg replacer, vanilla, and almond extract. Combine the dry and wet ingredients. Spoon onto a nonstick cookie sheet, and bake for 10 to 15 minutes.

½ cup fructose or brown rice syrup
½ cup non-dairy margarine
Egg replacer equivalent to 1 egg
1 teaspoon vanilla
½ teaspoon almond extract

Per cookie: Calories 129, Protein 1 g, Fat 6 g, Carbohydrates 17 g

Almond Rice Pudding

Yield: 8 servings

4 cups soymilk
3½ tablespoons fructose
¾ cup uncooked long grain brown
    rice

Bring the soymilk to a boil in a heavy-bottomed, 2-quart saucepan, then turn down to a simmer. Add the fructose and rice. Allow to simmer gently for 45 minutes, stirring occasionally so the mixture doesn't stick to the bottom of the pan.

¾ cup chopped almonds
¼ cup cherry juice
2 teaspoons vanilla
1 cup chilled almond milk
Black cherry concentrate

Remove from the heat and add the almonds, cherry juice, and vanilla. Set aside to cool. Whip the almond milk in a chilled bowl with a wire whisk until it thickens. Fold it into the cooled rice mixture. Spoon into a serving bowl, and chill. Top with black cherry concentrate before serving.

Per serving: Calories 25, Protein 7 g, Fat 9 g, Carbohydrates 28 g

Bread Pudding

Yield: 8 servings

When cooking with citrus peel, be sure to use organic produce, as the non-organic fruit has been sprayed with chemicals that remain in the rind.

Preheat the oven to 300°F. Place the bread in a bowl. Heat the non-dairy milk, sweetener, and orange peel together. Pour over the bread and soak for 15 minutes.

4 cups cubed whole grain bread
3 cups non-dairy milk
1 cup date sugar, or 6 tablespoons molasses
2 teaspoons dried organic orange peel

Add the remaining ingredients to the bread mixture, and mix thoroughly. Bake for 1½ hours, or until the pudding has set. Serve hot or cold with rice milk, if desired.

1 medium apple, chopped
1 cup melted non-dairy margarine
¼ cup chopped dates
¼ cup raisins
1 teaspoon cinnamon

Per serving: Calories 419, Protein 4 g, Fat 31 g, Carbohydrates 33 g

Carob Mousse

Yield: 4 servings

4 oz. carob chunks
¼ cup non-dairy margarine
2 tablespoons soymilk or almond
   milk
1 tablespoon liquid sweetener
1 teaspoon vanilla extract
double recipe Tofu Whipped Cream,
   p. 127

Melt the carob and margarine with the soymilk and liquid sweetener in the top of a double boiler until the mixture is well blended. Allow to cool. Fold gently with the extract into the whipped cream. Chill before serving.

Per serving: Calories 434, Protein 13 g, Fat 16 g, Carbohydrates 59 g

Maple Syrup Cake

Yield: 12 servings

When cooking with citrus peel, be sure to use organic produce, as the non-organic fruit has been sprayed with chemicals that remain in the rind.

Preheat the oven to 350°F. Beat the egg replacer well. Mix the maple syrup or other liquid sweetener, grain coffee, vanilla, and add the oil, if using.

Egg replacer equivalent to 3 eggs
1 cup maple syrup or liquid sweetener of your choice
1 cup boiled grain coffee (Pero or Roastaroma)
Dash of vanilla extract
2 tablespoons safflower oil (optional)

Sift together the dry ingredients, and add to the beaten egg replacer mixture. Sprinkle the bottom of an oiled 9 x 13-inch pan with the sliced almonds, and spoon in the cake batter. Bake for 40 minutes, or until a toothpick inserted in the center comes out clean.

Dry Ingredients:
3¼ cups whole grain flour,
    or 1½ cups soy flour plus 1¾ cups whole grain flour
2 teaspoons baking powder
1 teaspoon baking soda
1 teaspoon powdered ginger
1 teaspoon cinnamon
1 teaspoon nutmeg
1 teaspoon freshly grated organic orange and/or lemon rind
Allspice and cloves to taste (optional)

½ cup sliced blanched almonds

Per serving: Calories 300, Protein 6 g, Fat 4 g, Carbohydrates 61 g

Middle Eastern Date and Banana Dessert

Yield: 6 to 8 servings

This is a marvelous, rich dessert!

4-5 large ripe bananas, thinly sliced
½ lb. pitted dates, cut in halves
  (about 2 cups)
½ cup coarsely chopped walnuts
  (optional)

In a serving dish, arrange alternate layers of thinly sliced bananas and dates. Sprinkle some of the chopped walnuts on top of each layer of dates.

1-1½ cups non-dairy milk

Pour the non-dairy milk over the other ingredients, and chill for several hours. The milk will soak into the fruit and give it a soft, slightly sticky texture.

Per serving: Calories 171, Protein 2 g, Fat 1 g, Carbohydrates 38 g

Round Halvah

Yield: 4 servings

½ cup tahini
½ cup finely ground date sugar,
  or ¼ cup maple syrup
¼ cup ground almonds or coconut
  flakes
1 teaspoon vanilla
Powdered almonds or coconut

Mix all the ingredients together, and mold into balls. Roll in the powdered almonds or coconut, and refrigerate.

Per serving: Calories 280, Protein 9 g, Fat 15 g, Carbohydrates 24 g

Glossary

Agar flakes: A tasty, vegetable-based gel made from seaweed that will set at room temperature.

Arrowroot: A white vegetable starch powder from the arrowroot plant which can be used for thickening. Use half as much arrowroot as you would cornstarch, and dissolve it in cool water before adding it to hot liquids. It does not have to boil to thicken.

Asafoetida or hing: A pungent spice commonly used in East Indian cooking. It has a flavor similar to garlic. If used when cooking beans, it will alleviate problems with gas often associated with eating beans.

Brown rice syrup: A liquid sweetener made from brown rice that has been only lightly polished, so it retains many of the nutrients found in the whole grain. Rice syrup has a light flavor and tends not to give one the extreme energy surge that is often experienced after eating highly refined sweeteners.

Chinese black mushrooms: These are often found dried in Oriental or specialty food stores. When rehydrated with boiling water, they are chewy and mild-flavored.

Dulse: A red sea vegetable grown in northern oceans and especially popular in the British Isles and Canada. It can be eaten fresh in salads or dried in breads, soups, and relishes. Dulse is an excellent source of iodine and other minerals, protein, and vitamins.

Egg replacer: Mashed bananas, blended tofu, applesauce, a little additional baking powder, oil, or water can often replace the moistening and/or leavening power of eggs in a recipe for baked goods. Also, Ener-G Egg Replacer is a good commercial brand.

Fructose: This type of sugar, found in fruits and honey, is available as crystals or syrup. Although sweeter than refined cane sugar, it is thought that fructose is not absorbed as quickly into the bloodstream, so it does not raise blood sugar and insulin levels as drastically.

Herbamere seasoning: A dry seasoning prepared from fresh, organically grown herbs and sea salt. From a special recipe from famous naturopath Dr. A. Vogel.

Jicama: A round tuber favored in Mexican cooking, jicama has a bland flavor that ranges from something similar to apples to that of raw potatoes. The brown skin of the jicama should be peeled, then the firm white flesh can be used fresh in salads or added to stir fries, similar to how water chestnuts are used.

Kelp: Also known as laminaria, kelp can be found as a powder or dried. It adds a salty flavor to foods, as well as a wide range of minerals.

Miso: A thick, salty paste, originating in Japan, used as a flavoring. It is made by fermenting soybeans and/or grains, and can range from dark and "beefy" flavored to light tan and mildly "cheesy." Add it at the end of the cooking time; do not boil it or many of the beneficial enzymes it contains will be destroyed.

Rice polishings: The inner layers of the rice bran along with bits of germ that are removed when the rice is polished. Rice polishings are highly nutritious and have a lightly cheesy flavor.

Soy isolate: Soy powder from which most of the carbohydrates and fat have been removed, leaving a highly concentrated source of soy proteins. It can easily be added to baked goods, pancakes, shakes, and creamy soups to supplement the soy protein content.

Tahini: A nut butter made from ground hulled sesame seeds. The seeds can either be roasted or raw before grinding. Tahini gives a delicious flavor to dressings and sauces, and can replace oil or eggs in baked goods.

Tamari: Most tamari sold in this country is actually shoyu, a liquid flavoring made from soybeans, wheat, salt, and water. If you have a wheat allergy, look for wheat-free brands.

Tempeh: A white cake of soybeans (or combination of beans and grains) that has been bound together with the thin fibers of a variety of mushroom. Tempeh has a light, fragrant aroma. Look for it in the frozen food section of most natural foods stores.

Tofu: Tofu is a delicately flavored, custard-like block made in various densities from curdled soymilk. Soft tofu is the best choice for blended recipes; firm or extra-firm is used whenever you need the tofu to hold together, in stir frys, salads, or sandwiches. If your tofu is not in aseptic packaging, you need to store it in water in your refrigerator where it will keep for up to a week.

Whole grain flour: A blend of any one of a number of wheat-free flours, such as amaranth, barley, buckwheat, corn, millet, oat, quinoa, rice, rye, tapioca, and teff. Kamut and spelt are ancient forms of cultivated wheat that can also be tolerated by many people with wheat allergies.

Index

All the recipes in this book are wheat-, egg-, and dairy-free. Check in these general sections for combinations you can make without problem foods:

The following recipes are also free of the following ingredients:

No Corn:

No Corn (cont.)

No Nightshade Vegetables (tomatoes, potatoes, peppers, eggplant):

No Nightshade Vegetables (cont.)

Ask your store to carry these vegan books, or you may order directly from:

The Book Publishing Company
P.O. Box 99
Summertown, TN 38483

20-Minutes To Dinner $12.95
Chef Neil's International Vegetarian Cookbook 5.00
Cooking With PETA 14.95
Ecological Cooking: Recipes to Save the Planet 10.95
Fabulous Beans 9.95
Fat Free and Easy 10.00
Foods Can Save Your Life 9.95
Foods That Cause You To Loose Weight 12.95
Health Promoting Cookbook 12.95
Holiday Diet Book 7.95
Lighten Up! with Louise Hagler 11.95
Nutritional Yeast Cookbook 9.95
Peaceful Palate 15.00
Solar Cooking 8.95
Soyfoods Cookery 9.95
Soups On! 10.95
The Sprout Garden 8.95
Table for Two 12.95
Uncheese Cookbook 11.95
Vegan Vittles 11.95
Vegetarian Cooking For People With Diabetes 10.95

Or call: 1-800-695-2241
Please add $2.50 per book for shipping

If you need help organizing a more healthful diet for weight loss or increased energy, be sure to order Dr. Rettner's video *The Ultimate Diet*. If you are suffering from PMS, his video *End PMS Now* gives a complete description of the four types of PMS, as well as the diet, vitamins, minerals, and Chinese herbs used in successfully treating the symptoms. To order, call 1-800-236-6899